AQA GCSE

ENGLISH AND ENGLISH LANGUAGE
Achieve a C

Peter Buckroyd (Chapters 1–14 & 16)
Highly experienced Senior Examiner

Adrian Beard (Chapter 15)
Highly experienced Moderator: Speaking and Listening

www.pearsonschools.co.uk

✓ Free online support
✓ Useful weblinks
✓ 24 hour online ordering

0845 630 22 22

Heinemann

Part of Pearson

Heinemann is an imprint of Pearson Education Limited, a company incorporated in England and Wales, having its registered office at Edinburgh Gate, Harlow, Essex, CM20 2JE. Registered company number: 872828

www.pearsonschools.co.uk

Heinemann is the registered trademark of Pearson Education Limited

Text © Pearson Education Limited 2010

First published 2010

14 13 12 11
10 9 8 7 6 5 4 3

British Library Cataloguing in Publication Data
A catalogue record for this book is available from the British Library on request.

ISBN 978 0 435118 14 3

Websites
The websites used in this book were correct and up-to-date at the time of publication. It is essential for tutors to preview each website before using it in class so as to ensure that the URL is still accurate, relevant and appropriate.

Designed and produced by Kamae Design, Oxford
Cover design by Wooden Ark Studios, Leeds
Original illustrations © Pearson Education Limited 2010
Illustrated by Kathryn Baker and Rory Walker
Picture research by Virginia Stroud-Lewis
Cover photo © Nikreates/Alamy
Printed in Malaysia (CTP-VP)

Acknowledgements
The author and publisher would like to thank the following individuals and organisations for permission to reproduce photographs:

ppiv-v Getty Images News; pp2-3 ©Alamy/vario images GmbH & Co. KG/Bernhard Classen; p4 Courtesy of The Advertising Archives; p6 Commercial Eye/Getty Images; pp8-9 Wayne HUTCHINSON/Alamy; p12 Courtesy of The Advertising Archives; p14 Francis Wong Chee Yen. Shutterstock; p15 Alamy/TavlikosPhoto MotorSports; pp16-17 Getty Images; p20 Bettmann/Corbis; p21 Young Family. Shutterstock; p23 VCL/Spencer Rowell/Getty Images; p24 WireImage. Getty Images; p25 (otter) MARK HICKEN/Alamy, (butterfly) George McCarthy/CORBIS; p27 Pearson Education Ltd. Jules Selmes; p30 Getty Images; p33 Pictorial Press Ltd/Alamy; pp34-35 News of the World/News Group Newspapers/NI Syndication; p39 Getty Images/Ian Walton; p40 Shutterstock/Ivonne Wierink; p41 Drive Images/Alamy; p43 ©Nicholas Hendrickx/Barcroft Media; pp46, 49 Londonstills.com/Alamy; p47 (Phil Neville) The Sun/News Group Newspapers/NI Syndication, (mansion) Manchester Evening News; pp50-51 Solent News and Photo Agency; p56 Ian Francis/Alamy; pp58-59 ©South West News Service; pp60-61 Ragdoll BBC Worldwide; p62 (town hall) ©Wikimedia Commons, (Queen) ©2009 The Press Association/ Anwar Hussein/EMPICS Entertainment; p67 Yellowj. Shutterstock; pp70-71 Brendan Howard.Shutterstock; p73 mashe. Shutterstock; pp80-81 Alamy/ National Trust Photo library/Jerry Harpur; pp82-83 ©Alamy/Mark J. Barrett; pp84-85 ©Education Photos; p89 Geoff Delderfield.Shutterstock; p90 ©Caters News Agency; p92 Photodisc. Keith Brofsky; p93 Alex Segre/Alamy; p95 Ace Stock Limited/Alamy; p99 Adams Picture Library t/a apl/Alamy; p101 PA Photos sport/Joe Giddens; p106 ©Shutterstock/ Thomas M Perkins; p107 Rex Features; p110 www.Cartoonstock.com; p111 Xavier MARCHANT. Shutterstock; p112 Jack Wild.Getty Images; p114 Rex Features; p116 Design Pics Inc; p117 Photodisc; p118 Getty Images; p121 Photodisc/Photolink/F. Schussler; p122 Pearson Education Ltd. Rob Judges; p128 Pearson Education Ltd. Gareth Boden; p130 (c)Getty Images/Jeff J Mitchell; p141 Alamy/Oxford Picture Library. Chris Andrews; pp144-145 London Media Pictures; p148 Woodfall/Photoshot/Erlend Haarberg; p149 Andrew Milligan/PA Archive/Press Association Images.

Every effort has been made to contact copyright holders of material reproduced in this book. Any omissions will be rectified in subsequent printings if notice is given to the publishers.

'Boost your pecs appeal' by Peta Bee, *The Times*, 8 December 2008, used with permission of NI Syndication; 'Cold, Aching Hands? Try Heat Therapy Gloves' *The Times*, 27 December 2008 advert provided by 20200DM; 'Make your money grow further' by Matt James, *News of the World*, 8 March 2009, used with permission of NI Syndication; Collins Dictionary and Thesaurus advert provided by Franklin & Consumer Products www.franklin-uk.co.uk; 'Dancing parrot mesmerises scientists' *www.orange. co.uk news pages*, used with permission Orange PR Golin Harris; 'Spike your blood with adrenalin' by Janie Omorogbe, *The Sun*, 6 March 2009, used with permission of NI Syndication; 'New toe job a woe job, Paula' by Vicki Orvice, *The Sun*, 6 March 2009, used by permission NI Syndication; 'Time to turn the cameras off Jade' by Carole Malone, *News of the World*, 8 March 2009, used with permission of NI Syndication; Photo of Carole Malone used with permission of NI Syndication; 'Hip-hop offers a new message by Ian Burrell,*The Independent*, 8 May 2009, used with permission of Independent News and Media Limited; 'Why a third wet summer would spell disaster for birds and bees' by Kaya Burgess, *The Times*, 27 December 2008, used with permission of NI Syndication; 'Let schools decide how to teach' *The Independent*, 9 December 2008, used with permission of Independent News and Media Limited; 'Taurus' prediction from 'Your Horoscope' by David Wells, *Daily Mirror*, 17 August 2009, used with permission of Mirrorpix; 'Perfect Rossi, MotoGP' by Dave Fern, *Daily Express*, 17 August 2009, used with kind permission of Dave Fern; 'The purest Icelandic cod liver oil' advert provided thanks to Healthspan, the UK's leading direct to consumer supplier of nutritional supplements; 'Ve are not amused' by Robert Jobson, *News of the World*, 15 March 2009, used with permission NI Syndication; 'Lucky 13! Steve strikes as fans hurl missiles' by Bill Pierce *News of the World*, 15 March 2009, used with permission of NI Syndication; 'Higgins and Murphy set up Crucible cracker' by Darren Lewis, *Daily Mirror*, 4 May 2009, used with permission of Mirrorpix; 'The definitive guide to the ugliest cars ever: Toyota Scion XB' *www.orange.co.uk news pages*, used with permission of Orange PR Golin Harris; 'The fantastic Mr Fly' by Ross McGuinness *Metro*, 4 November 2007, used with permission of Solo Syndication; 'DLR to benefit from massive 2012 Games investment' *Metro*, 10 December 2008, used with permission of Solo Synducation; 'You can sell this thing if it ain't got that bling' by Ben Ashford, *The Sun*, 22 November 2008, used with permission of NI Syndication; 'The above-par birdie' by Ross McGuinness, *Metro*, 18 March 2009, used with permission of Solo Syndication; 'Six of the best - Headbands, chosen by Claire Foster, accessories editor of WGSN' *The Guardian*, 1 May 2009, used with permission of Guardian News and Media Ltd 2009; Headline 'Phil the cracks! Players turning on Scolari' by Shaun Curtis and Paul Jiggins, *The Sun*, 6 December 2008, used with permission of NI Syndication; Headline 'Vince swims against the sea of sewage' by Kelvin MacKenzie, *The Sun*, 14 May 2009, used with permission of NI Syndication; Headline: 'Bring back the beaver - he will save money and clean our rivers' by Valerie Elliott, *The Times*, 8 March 2009, used with permission of NI Syndication; Headline: 'I Canute believe it, my home is saved' by Aidan McGurran, *Daily Mirror*, 6 December 2008, used by permission of Mirrorpix; 'It's a plant, officer' by John Coles *The Sun*, 6 December 2008, used with permission of NI Syndication; 'Dopes!' by Geoffrey Lakeman, *Daily Mirror*, 6 December 2008, used by permission of Mirrorpix; 'Kids TV gets touchy-feely' by Victoria Richards, *Daily Star*, 19 May 2009, used with permission of Northern and Shell Media Publications; 'Union Jackasses' by Jerry Lawton, *Daily Star*, 19 May 2009, used with permission of Northern and Shell Media Publications; 'Sport of Queens' *The Times*, 14 March 2009, used with permission of NI Syndication; 'Lanhydrock' from 'Enjoy a great day out in Cornwall. Beautiful and inspiring places to visit in 2008', *National Trust leaflet*, used with kind permission of Liz Luck/National Trust; 'We're worth every penny' by Jay Curson, *The Guardian*,19 October 2002 used with permission of Guardian News and Media Limited, 2009; 'Grabbing a bite to eat' by Miles Erwin, *Metro*, 30 April 2009, used with permission of Solo Syndication; 'Rhine Valley by Eurostar' advert, *The Guardian*, 27 August 2009 used by permission of Guardian News and Media Limited 2009; From 'Beautiful Britain: Need an autumn break? Look closer to home and you'll be pleasantly surprised' by Chris Alden *Daily Telegraph*, 18 October 2008.Used with permission ©Telegraph Media Group Ltd 2007; 'Flight' from *The Habit of Loving* by Doris Lessing. Copyright © 1957 Doris Lessing. Reprinted by kind permission of Jonathan Clowes Ltd. London, on behalf of Doris Lessing; 'After 400 years, stepladders are banned from Oxford's library' *Daily Mail*, 9 May 2009, used with permission of Solo Syndication; 'We are up for the cup' *Daily Star*, 19 May 2008, used with permission of Northern and Shell Media Publications; 'Guess which one lowers your cholesterol?' *Benecol advert*, with thanks to McNeil Nutritionals. Copyright © McNeil Nutrionals 2009; '2012 The Slummer Olympics' by Daniel Jones, *The People*, 28 December 2008, used with permission of Mirrorpix; 'Bring back the beaver - he will save money and clean our rivers,' by Valerie Elliott, *The Times*, 18 March 2009, used with permission of NI Syndication; 'Seasonal stray-dog crisis comes early as families abandon pets to save cash' by Fiona Hamilton, *The Times*, 16 December 2008, used with permission of NI Syndication; Extract from *The Source*, Copyright © Gillian Clarke 2008, reprinted by permission of Carcanet Press Limited.

Contents

Introduction

From Peter Buckroyd

This book is designed to help students raise their achievement in the AQA GCSE English and GCSE English Language exam. It is tailored to the requirements of the specification to help students achieve grades D–B. It also includes an outline of the specifications.

The book breaks down the Assessment Objectives into their component parts. It then provides students with:

▶ guidance and teaching on the key skills that make the difference between a D, C and B

▶ examples of students' work at grades D, C and B with examiner comments

▶ activities that allow students to reflect and improve on their learning

▶ the relevant mark scheme descriptors together with guidance on what the examiners are looking for

▶ tips from an experienced Chief Examiner on how to move from a D to a C and then to a B.

The approach that this book uses comes out of many years of examining experience and out of workshops, training sessions and revision courses with teachers and students. It can be used with confidence by all students who have the potential to move from a grade D to a C and then to a B.

The book also includes a section on the Spoken Language Study that provides you with activities and possible approaches to this new requirement of the English Language specification.

I hope you enjoy using it and wish you every success!

Peter Buckroyd

How is the book structured?

The books is broken down into four sections: ▶ Reading ▶ Writing ▶ Spoken Language Study ▶ Exam practice.

The Reading and Writing sections are divided into chapters. These chapters relate either to complete Assessment Objectives, elements of Assessments Objectives or helpful deconstruction of the Assessment Objectives.

Each chapter is then broken down into lessons, each of which opens with its own learning objectives ('My learning'). These introduce the skills, and then through stepped activities and examiner comments lead to a final activity that allows students to tackle an exam-style question.

Most chapters conclude with Grade Studio, which provides an opportunity to read sample student answers and examiner comments on the final activity in the chapter. These can be read by students before or after they grade themselves in the 'Peer/Self-assessment' activity.

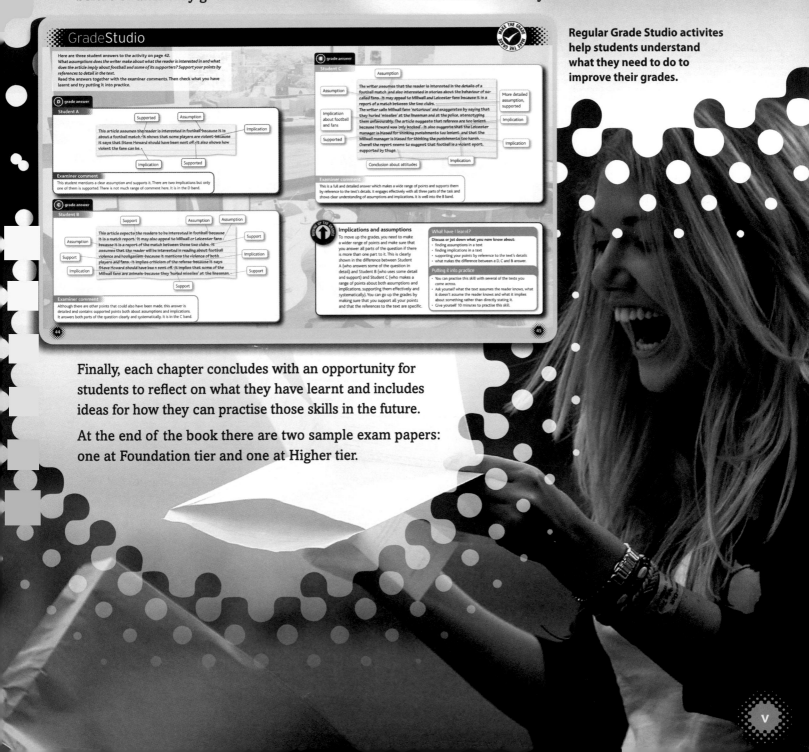

Regular Grade Studio activites help students understand what they need to do to improve their grades.

Finally, each chapter concludes with an opportunity for students to reflect on what they have learnt and includes ideas for how they can practise those skills in the future.

At the end of the book there are two sample exam papers: one at Foundation tier and one at Higher tier.

The AQA GCSE English and English Language specifications

This book is predominantly for students taking the AQA GCSE English and English Language Unit 1 exam. Chapters 1 to 14 provide activities and assessment practice for the exam, while chapter 16 includes sample exam papers. The book is also useful for those students tackling the new Spoken Language Study – chapter 15 explains the requirements of this new area of study as well as providing a wealth of activities to get students started.

An overview of the specifications for both GCSE English and GCSE English Language can be found below and on the following pages.

GCSE English and GCSE English Language Unit 1

Here is an overview of the Unit 1 exam, which is common to both GCSE English and GCSE English Language.

What is this unit worth?	40% of the total marks
How long is this exam?	2 hours
What is Section A of the exam?	Reading responses to non-fiction texts
What is Section A worth?	20% of the total marks
How long should you spend on Section A?	1 hour
What is Section B of the exam?	Two Writing responses
What is Section B worth?	20% of the total marks
How long should you spend on Section B?	1 hour

For full details, see the corresponding Heinemann Teacher Guide and AQA specifications.

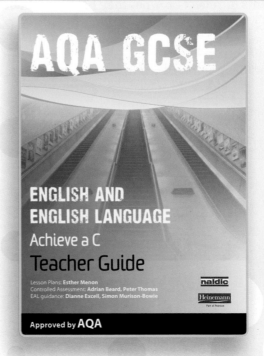

Unit 1: Resources from Heinemann

▶ Student Books – as well as this book, further grade-banded student books are available from Heinemann to support the teaching of Unit 1. We have developed the *Achieve an A** and *Basic Skills* student books so that you can pitch the learning at the appropriate level for your students.

▶ Teacher Guide – full colour lesson plans can be found in the corresponding Heinemann Teacher Guide, written by experienced author and LA Adviser, Esther Menon. These lesson plans make use of and reference the BBC footage and other resources in the ActiveTeach CD-ROM as well as providing support for EAL students written by NALDIC (professional body of EAL teachers and advisors).

Each Teacher Guide is accompanied by a CD-ROM which contains the lesson plans as Word files, so they are fully customisable. If you have purchased both components these lesson plans can be uploaded into ActiveTeach.

> **Explains which assessment objectives are being covered.**

> **Advice from NALDIC on how to help EAL students access the content for each lesson.**

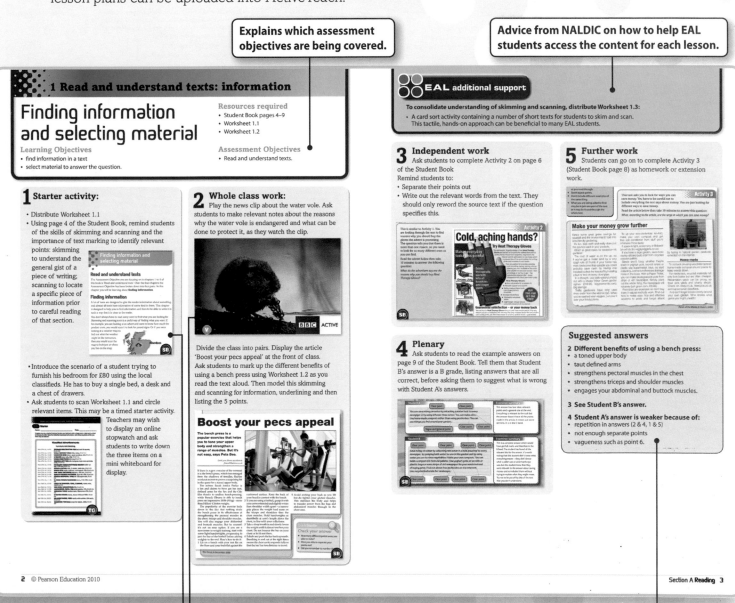

> **Full colour lesson plans show exactly where resources from the student book and ActiveTeach could be used.**

> **Answers to student book activities are provided throughout.**

▶ ActiveTeach CD-ROM – onscreen version of the student book together with BBC footage and other assets including: Grade Studio grade-improvement activities; additional video footage and worksheets. ActiveTeach allows you to play and customise lessons and import your own resources.

A wealth of digital resources, including exclusive BBC footage.

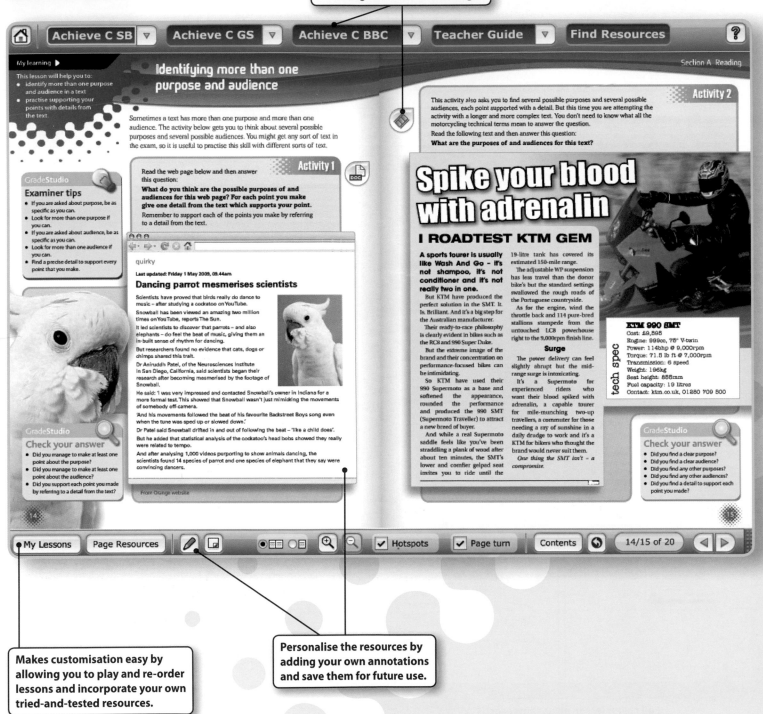

Makes customisation easy by allowing you to play and re-order lessons and incorporate your own tried-and-tested resources.

Personalise the resources by adding your own annotations and save them for future use.

GCSE English and GCSE English Language Unit 2

This is the Speaking and Listening Unit and is the same for GCSE English and GCSE English Language. It is worth 20% of the total marks and is assessed through Controlled Assessment. For full details, see the AQA specifications.

GCSE English and GCSE English Language Unit 3

There is commonality here between GCSE English and GCSE English Language, but for clarity they have been set out separately below. Unit 3 is assessed through Controlled Assessment and is worth 40% of the total marks.

GCSE English: Understanding and producing creative texts

This comprises:

- Understanding creative texts (literary reading) – worth 20% of the total marks

- Producing creative texts (creative writing) – worth 20% of the total marks.

GCSE English Language: Understanding spoken and written texts and writing creatively

This comprises:

- Extended reading – worth 15% of the total marks

- Creative writing – worth 15% of the total marks

- Spoken Language Study – worth 10% of the total marks.

Controlled Assessment resources from Heinemann

This student book includes a section on the new Spoken Language Study. The Teacher Guides include comprehensive support for each of the three areas of Controlled Assessment. Written by experienced examiners and coursework moderators, each Controlled Assessment section includes:

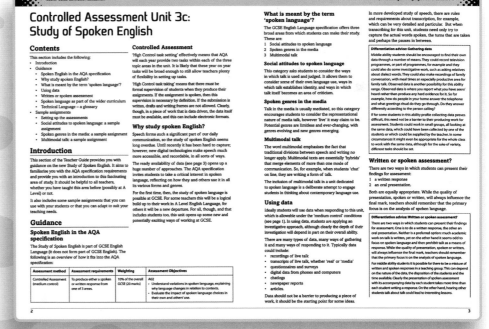

- advice on the impact of the shift from coursework to Controlled Assessment

- specific guidance on all of the task types in the AQA Controlled Assessment Task Bank

- exemplar answers showing what kinds of responses you might expect to see

- suggestions for how you might approach, timetable and differentiate the Controlled Assessments.

For full details, see the corresponding Heinemann Teacher Guide or AQA specifications.

Section A Reading

Introduction

This section aims to encourage you to develop your reading skills in response to a range of texts. The teaching, texts, activities and tips are all focused on helping you achieve the best grade you can in your exam.

This part of your course encourages you to look at the range and use of media and non-fiction texts. These texts appear everywhere in daily life and the selection in this book should help you to see and appreciate how the English language is presented and used. The texts chosen in this book also aim to improve your reading skills and prepare you for the requirements of the exam.

Reading media and non-fiction texts is something you do every day without necessarily realising it. This book will help contribute to your understanding, enjoyment and analyses of texts.

The skills that you will work on in this book can be applied to any texts that you read, whether these are in print form or onscreen. You don't just have to rely on English lessons to practise these skills.

This book focuses on the skills that you need to be successful in the exam. You will find a wide range of different kinds of texts and activities based around the sorts of questions that you might get in the exam.

Assessment Objectives

The Assessment Objectives underpin everything you will learn about and be tested upon. It is vital that you understand what these are asking of you. So, here are the Assessment Objectives that relate to your Reading exam together with comments to help you understand what they are.

▶ Read and understand texts, selecting material appropriate to purpose, collating from different sources and making comparisons and cross-references as appropriate.

▶ Explain and evaluate how writers use linguistic, grammatical, structural and presentational features to achieve effects and engage and influence the reader.

This Assessment Objective is asking you to show that you:
- understand what you read
- answer the question by selecting appropriate material from the text to support the points that you make
- select texts, when asked, from which to answer the question and make comparisons between texts.

This Assessment Objective is asking you to show that you can identify each of the following and then explain what effect they have on the reader:
- a range of features of language
- features of grammar
- structural devices
- presentational devices.

Examiner and student concerns

To help you improve your grades it is helpful to know what concerns examiners and students most about the Reading section of the exam. Below is a list of some of the concerns that they have.

What concerns examiners?

▶ Failure to focus on the task.

▶ Giving several examples of the same thing rather than looking for a range of things.

▶ Spending more time on questions with few marks than on questions with more marks.

▶ Missing questions out altogether.

What concerns students?

▶ I haven't got time to think before I write.

▶ How many points should I make?

▶ How much should I write?

▶ I'd rather do one question properly than spend my time equally between the questions.

My learning ▶

This lesson will help you to:
- find information in a text
- select material to answer the question.

Finding information and selecting material

Many texts are designed to give the reader information about something, and almost all texts have information of some kind in them. This chapter is designed to help you find information and then to be able to write it in such a way that it is clear to the reader.

Skimming and scanning

You don't always have to read every word to find what you are looking for. **Skimming** and **scanning** texts is a useful way of finding what you want. If, for example, you are looking at an advert and want to know how much the product costs, you would scan it to look for pound signs.

Where would you look on the weather map opposite to find out what the weather might be like tomorrow?

GradeStudio

Examiner tips

In the exam you are likely to be asked to:
- find specific points in a text
- find, copy and number them
- select the main points
- put the main points in your own words
- show that you can follow the sequence of points being made.

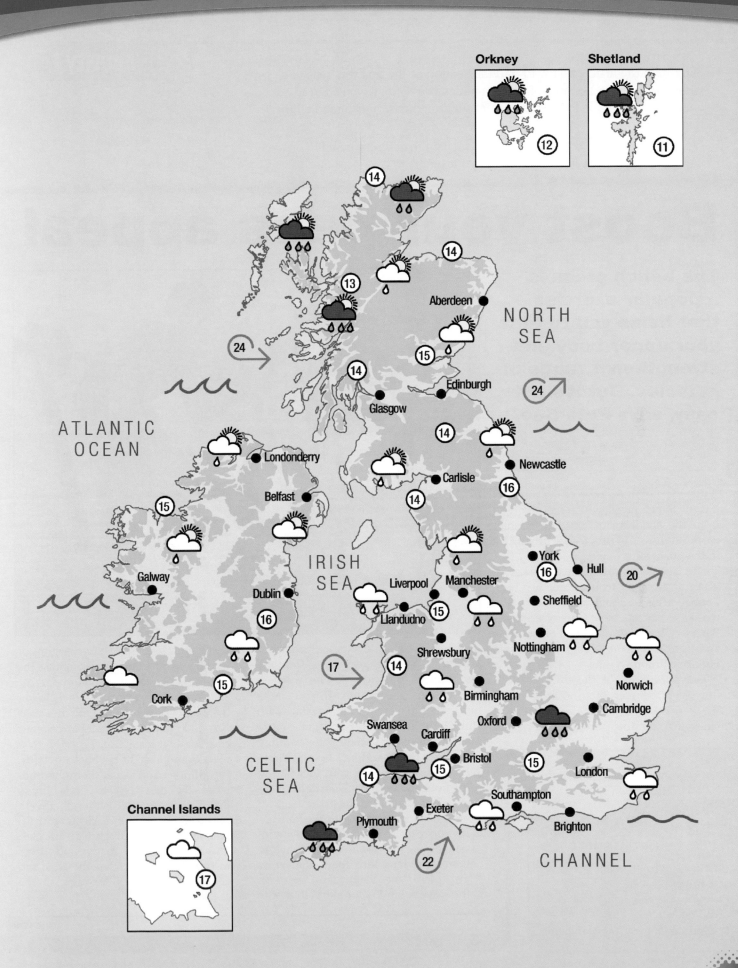

1 Skim read the article below to find the section of the text that tells you what the different benefits of using a bench press are. If you want to check that you have found the correct section, then you can read all the text carefully.

2 Once you have found the correct section, list the different benefits of using a bench press. Number each of your points.

Boost your pecs appeal

The bench press is a popular exercise that helps you to tone your upper body and strengthen a range of muscles. But it's not easy, says Peta Bee.

Send your fitness questions to fitness@thetimes.co.uk

If there is a gym exercise of the moment it is the bench press, which has emerged from the shadows of trendier, flashier workout moves to prove a surprising hit in the quest for a toned upper body.

The actress Sarah Jessica Parker is a fan and claims to have got her taut, defined arms for the *Sex and the City* film thanks to endless bench-pressing, while Barack Obama is able to bench press an impressive 200lb (91kg) – more than Hillary Clinton weighs.

The popularity of the exercise boils down to the fact that nothing rivals the bench press in its effectiveness at strengthening the pectoral muscles in the chest, triceps and shoulder muscles. You will also engage your abdominal and buttock muscles. But be warned: it's not an easy option. If you are a newcomer to weight training, start with some light handweights, progressing to just the bar of the barbell before adding weights to the end. Here's how to do it:

1 Lie on a bench with your feet flat on the floor and your back flat against the cushioned surface. Keep the back of your head in contact with the bench.

2 If you are using a barbell, grasp it with your arms extended and slightly wider than shoulder width apart – a narrow grip places the weight load more on the triceps and shoulders than the chest muscles. Hold handweights or dumbbells at arm's length above the chest, in line with your collarbone.

3 Take a deep breath in and slowly lower the weight until it almost touches your chest. Do not bounce the bar on your chest or let it rest there.

4 Exhale and push the bar back upwards. Breathing in and out at the right times means the chest cavity expands fully so that the bar has less distance to travel.

5 Avoid arching your back as you lift but do tighten your gluteal muscles. This stabilises the body and helps to transfer power from the legs and abdominal muscles through to the chest area.

THE TIMES

This is similar to Activity 1. You are looking through the text to find reasons why you should buy the gloves the advert is promoting. The question tells you that there is more than one reason, so you need to look for as many different ones as you can find.

Read the advert below and then answer the following question:

What do the advertisers say are the reasons why you should buy Heat Therapy Gloves?

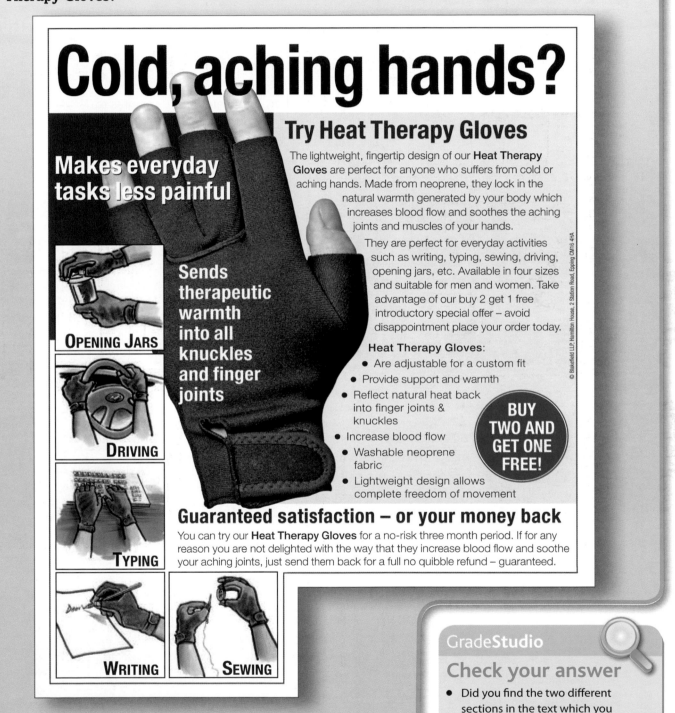

Cold, aching hands?

Makes everyday tasks less painful

OPENING JARS

DRIVING

TYPING

WRITING

SEWING

Sends therapeutic warmth into all knuckles and finger joints

Try Heat Therapy Gloves

The lightweight, fingertip design of our **Heat Therapy Gloves** are perfect for anyone who suffers from cold or aching hands. Made from neoprene, they lock in the natural warmth generated by your body which increases blood flow and soothes the aching joints and muscles of your hands.

They are perfect for everyday activities such as writing, typing, sewing, driving, opening jars, etc. Available in four sizes and suitable for men and women. Take advantage of our buy 2 get 1 free introductory special offer – avoid disappointment place your order today.

Heat Therapy Gloves:
- Are adjustable for a custom fit
- Provide support and warmth
- Reflect natural heat back into finger joints & knuckles
- Increase blood flow
- Washable neoprene fabric
- Lightweight design allows complete freedom of movement

BUY TWO AND GET ONE FREE!

© Blakefield LLP, Hamilton House, 2 Station Road, Epping CM16 4HA

Guaranteed satisfaction – or your money back

You can try our **Heat Therapy Gloves** for a no-risk three month period. If for any reason you are not delighted with the way that they increase blood flow and soothe your aching joints, just send them back for a full no quibble refund – guaranteed.

GradeStudio

Check your answer
- Did you find the two different sections in the text which you needed in order to be able to answer the question fully?
- Did you separate your points out?
- Did you write them clearly?

My learning ▶

This lesson will help you to:
● practise an exam-style question
● assess your answer by looking at other responses.

Assessment practice

Now you are going to have a go at an exam-style question. Attempt the activity in the time suggested and then complete the Peer/Self-assessment activity that follows.

Activity 1

This task asks you to look for ways you can save money. You have to be careful not to include everything the text says about money. You are just looking for different ways to save money.

Read the article below and then take 10 minutes to answer this question:

What, according to the article, are the ways in which you can save money?

Make your money grow further

Fancy some great green savings for yourself and the environment? Get into eco-friendly gardening.

It's fun, less work and really does put the pounds back in your pockets.

Which is great news for recession-hit gardens!

The cost of water is on the up, so if you've got a meter (and by a very rough rule of thumb if your home has more bedrooms than people you could probably save cash by having one installed) collect the free stuff by installing a butt or two on every downpipe.

In a drought, use bath-water pumped out with a cheap Water Green garden siphon (£19.99, biggreensmile.com). Big savings!

Thrifty gardeners have long used rinse-water from the kitchen too. When you've washed your veggies, just pour it over your thirsty plants.

To up your eco-credentials ten-fold, make your own compost and get free soil conditioner from stuff you'd otherwise throw away.

If space is tight, a wormery or Bokashi bin will do (try wigglywigglers.co.uk).

GradeStudio

Examiner tips

- In the exam always underline the points in pencil as you read through.
- Don't repeat points.
- Don't include different examples of the same thing.
- What you are being asked to find may be in just one part of the text or it may be found through the whole text.

Peer/Self-assessment activity

1 Check your answer to Activity 1.
   - Did you include all the different points you could find?
   - Have you avoided repetition and using more than one example of the same thing?
   - Is your answer clear and detailed?
2 Now grade your answer to Activity 1 using the mark scheme below. You will need to be careful and precise in your marking. Before you do this, you might like to read some sample answers to this activity on pages 10 and 11.

D
- identifies two or more main points
- unstructured response
- some extra material.

C
- clear attempt to answer question
- several points made
- most material chosen to focus on ways to save money.

B
- clear and effective attempt to engage with activity
- range of relevant points
- clear understanding of material.

NEWS OF THE WORLD

If you have a large garden, save more money still and build a bin from recycled wooden pallets.

Seeds aren't fussy whether they're sown in yoghurt pots, loo-roll inners or plastic veg supermarket trays, so start collecting. Just be sure there are drainage holes in the base. With a Paper Potter, you can make biodegradable pots from strips of old newspaper. Simply plant out the whole thing, the newspaper will rot away (just-green.com, £8.99).

Pesticides are expensive so don't buy them if natural methods work. Find out how to make easy, free and effective solutions to pests and fungal attack by typing in 'natural garden pesticide remedies' on the internet.

Home-made

To cut back on using weed killer spread home-made compost around plants to keep weeds down.

For hardscape, recycled materials not only look better but are often cheaper. Reclamation yards can be pricey, so trawl junk yards and charity shops. Check on ebay. co.uk, freecycle.co.uk and supermarket classifieds.

And don't forget to look closely around your own garden. Who knows what gems you might unearth!

GradeStudio

Here are three student answers to the activity from page 8:

What, according to the article, are the ways in which you can save money?

Read the answers together with the examiner comments. Then check what you have learnt and try putting it into practice.

D grade answer

Student A

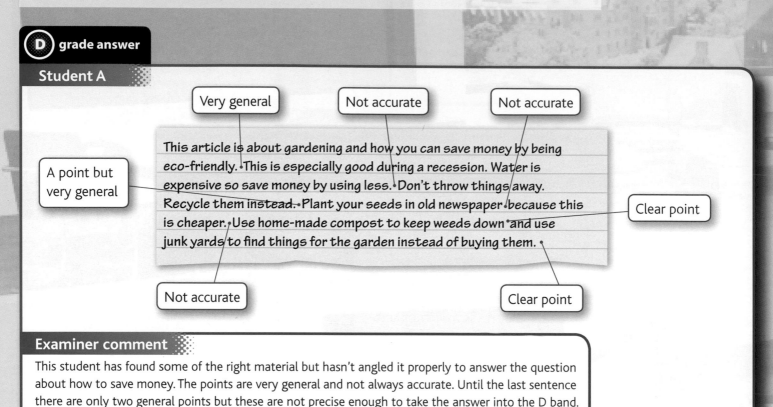

Very general

Not accurate

Not accurate

A point but very general

Clear point

Not accurate

Clear point

This article is about gardening and how you can save money by being eco-friendly. This is especially good during a recession. Water is expensive so save money by using less. Don't throw things away. Recycle them instead. Plant your seeds in old newspaper because this is cheaper. Use home-made compost to keep weeds down and use junk yards to find things for the garden instead of buying them.

Examiner comment

This student has found some of the right material but hasn't angled it properly to answer the question about how to save money. The points are very general and not always accurate. Until the last sentence there are only two general points but these are not precise enough to take the answer into the D band. The last sentence, however, lifts the answer into D with two clear, relevant points made.

C grade answer

Student B

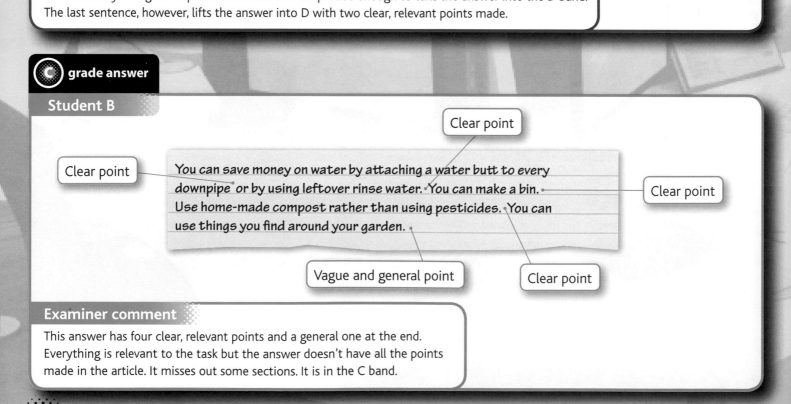

Clear point

Clear point

Clear point

You can save money on water by attaching a water butt to every downpipe or by using leftover rinse water. You can make a bin. Use home-made compost rather than using pesticides. You can use things you find around your garden.

Vague and general point

Clear point

Examiner comment

This answer has four clear, relevant points and a general one at the end. Everything is relevant to the task but the answer doesn't have all the points made in the article. It misses out some sections. It is in the C band.

B grade answer

Student C

Clear point

Clear point

Clear point

Clear point

Clear point

Save money on water by collecting rain water in a butt attached to every downpipe, by pumping bath water to use in the garden and by using water you use to rinse vegetables. Make your own compost. You can build a compost bin from old pallets. Use yoghurt pots or loo rolls or plastic trays or even strips of old newspaper for your seeds instead of buying pots. Find out about free pesticides on the internet. Use recycled materials for hardscape.

Clear point

Clear point

Clear point

Examiner comment

This is a complete answer which would have got full marks and is in the B band. The student has found all the relevant bits for the answer. It's worth noting that this student didn't know what everything meant – they didn't know what a pallet was or what hardscape was, but the student knew that they were relevant to the answer about saving money and so included them without trying to explain what they might mean. Try not to be put off by bits of the text that you don't understand.

Finding information

To move up the grades, you need to make a wider range of points and to be exact and specific in the points you make. This is clearly shown in the difference between Student A, Student B and Student C. To be sure of a C grade:

- find all the sections of the text which give you information for the question
- make sure that you include it all
- don't add material to your answer that doesn't answer the question.

What have I learnt?

Discuss or jot down what you now know about:

- finding information in texts
- separating the points out
- answering the question
- what makes the difference between grade D, C and B answers on understanding texts exam questions.

Putting it into practice

- You can practise this exercise with any information text you come across.
- Use any newspapers, magazines, pages from textbooks, letters and adverts.
- Give yourself about 10 minutes to practise this skill.

Identifying purpose and audience

What is purpose?

The **purpose** is the main reason for the text. For instance, the purpose of an advert is to sell the product to the kinds of people who would buy it, so it's important to make sure that it is as persuasive as possible.

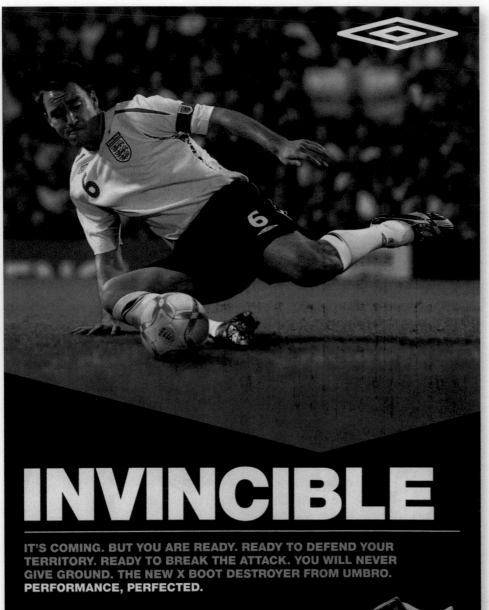

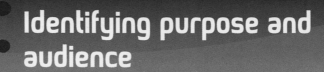

INVINCIBLE

IT'S COMING. BUT YOU ARE READY. READY TO DEFEND YOUR TERRITORY. READY TO BREAK THE ATTACK. YOU WILL NEVER GIVE GROUND. THE NEW X BOOT DESTROYER FROM UMBRO. PERFORMANCE, PERFECTED.

 onelove ◆ umbro.com

What is audience?

The **audience** is who the text is aimed at – who the reader is. An advert for trainers which has a picture of young people tells us who the audience is. An advert for trainers that shows runners tells us who it's aimed at. You can pick up clues from the pictures, the writing, the tone and the language about who the intended audience is.

Look at the advert on the left. What is its purpose and who do you think it is aimed at?

Activity 1 below is asking you to look at specific bits of the text in order to come to some conclusions about the purpose of the text and the audience it is aimed at. You need to include details which support the points you want to make in your answer.

Activity 1

Read the text below and then answer the following question:

What is the main purpose of and audience for this text? Support your points by reference to details in the text.

Reader offers

Collins Dictionary And Thesaurus

only £59.99
Price includes p&p

Features
- **Collins Desktop Plus English Dictionary with Spellchecker**
  Instant access to over 500,000 words and definitions
- Ability to search over 40 subjects including: Astronomy & Space, Biographies, Economics, Electronics, General sports, History, Literature, Medicine and Physics
- Phonetic spell correction for 180,000 words
- **Collins Concise Thesaurus** – Find over 250,000 synonyms and antonyms
- **Quotations from the Collins Thesaurus A–Z Complete and Unabridged** – Specially selected to add sparkle, interest and humour and give users instant access to the wit and wisdom of centuries. Over 3,500 quotations.

- **Collins Gem Bradford's Crossword Solver's Dictionary** – Look up over 120,000 crossword solutions.
- **Confusables®** – Identifies and defines commonly confused words, 'there', 'their' and 'they're'
- Crossword solver: Solve crossword puzzles by filling in missing letters in words
- Anagram solver: Turn a series of letters into a word
- Word builder: Build a word list with as many words as possible.
- **User List** – Create your own list of words to study
- **Additional references include:**
- Good Writing Guide from Collins Express Dictionary and Thesaurus, Write on Target from Collins Concise Dictionary, Rhetorically Speaking from Collins Compact Thesaurus, Word Power from Collins Concise Dictionary and Thesaurus, World in Action from Collins Paperback Dictionary, Language in Action from Collins Essential Dictionary and Thesaurus
- 13 Word Games from Collins Solutions Dictionary

Specifications
- Databank to store 100 names and numbers
- Calculator
- Metric and currency converter
- Databank to store names and phone numbers
- Local/world clock with 45 cities
- Dimensions: 13 x 10 x 1.3 cm
- 2 x CR2032 batteries (included)

My learning ▶

This lesson will help you to:
- identify more than one purpose and audience in a text
- practise supporting your points with details from the text.

Identifying more than one purpose and audience

Sometimes a text has more than one purpose and more than one audience. The activity below gets you to think about several possible purposes and several possible audiences. You might get any sort of text in the exam, so it is useful to practise this skill with different sorts of text.

Grade**Studio**

Examiner tips

- If you are asked about purpose, be as specific as you can.
- Look for more than one purpose if you can.
- If you are asked about audience, be as specific as you can.
- Look for more than one audience if you can.
- Find a precise detail to support every point that you make.

Activity 1

Read the web page below and then answer this question:

What do you think are the possible purposes of and audiences for this web page? For each point you make give one detail from the text which supports your point.

Remember to support each of the points you make by referring to a detail from the text.

Dancing parrot mesmerises scientists

Scientists have proved that birds really do dance to music – after studying a cockatoo on YouTube.

Snowball has been viewed an amazing two million times on YouTube, reports The Sun.

It led scientists to discover that parrots – and also elephants – do feel the beat of music, giving them an in-built sense of rhythm for dancing.

But researchers found no evidence that cats, dogs or chimps shared this trait.

Dr Aniruddh Patel, of the Neurosciences Institute in San Diego, California, said scientists began their research after becoming mesmerised by the footage of Snowball.

He said: 'I was very impressed and contacted Snowball's owner in Indiana for a more formal test. This showed that Snowball wasn't just mimicking the movements of somebody off-camera.

'And his movements followed the beat of his favourite Backstreet Boys song even when the tune was sped up or slowed down.'

Dr Patel said Snowball drifted in and out of following the beat – 'like a child does'.

But he added that statistical analysis of the cockatoo's head bobs showed they really were related to tempo.

And after analysing 1,000 videos purporting to show animals dancing, the scientists found 14 species of parrot and one species of elephant that they say were convincing dancers.

From Orange website

Grade**Studio**

Check your answer

- Did you manage to make at least one point about the purpose?
- Did you manage to make at least one point about the audience?
- Did you support each point you made by referring to a detail from the text?

Activity 2

This activity also asks you to find several possible purposes and several possible audiences, each point supported with a detail. But this time you are attempting the activity with a longer and more complex text. You don't need to know what all the motorcycling technical terms mean to answer the question.

Read the following text and then answer this question:

What are the purposes of and audiences for this text?

Spike your blood with adrenalin

I ROADTEST KTM GEM

A sports tourer is usually like Wash And Go – it's not shampoo, it's not conditioner and it's not really two in one.

But KTM have produced the perfect solution in the SMT. It. Is. Brilliant. And it's a big step for the Australian manufacturer.

Their ready-to-race philosophy is clearly evident in bikes such as the RC8 and 990 Super Duke.

But the extreme image of the brand and their concentration on performance-focused bikes can be intimidating.

So KTM have used their 990 Supermoto as a base and softened the appearance, rounded the performance and produced the 990 SMT (Supermoto Traveller) to attract a new breed of buyer.

And while a real Supermoto saddle feels like you've been straddling a plank of wood after about ten minutes, the SMT's lower and comfier gelpad seat invites you to ride until the 19-litre tank has covered its estimated 150-mile range.

The adjustable WP suspension has less travel than the donor bike's but the standard settings swallowed the rough roads of the Portuguese countryside.

As for the engine, wind the throttle back and 114 pure-bred stallions stampede from the untouched LC8 powerhouse right to the 9,000rpm finish line.

Surge

The power delivery can feel slightly abrupt but the mid-range surge is intoxicating.

It's a Supermoto for experienced riders who want their blood spiked with adrenalin, a capable tourer for mile-munching two-up travellers, a commuter for those needing a ray of sunshine in a daily drudge to work and it's a KTM for bikers who thought the brand would never suit them.

One thing the SMT isn't – a compromise.

tech spec

KTM 990 SMT
Cost: £9,595
Engine: 999cc, 75° V-twin
Power: 114bhp @ 9,000rpm
Torque: 71.5 lb ft @ 7,000rpm
Transmission: 6 speed
Weight: 196kg
Seat height: 855mm
Fuel capacity: 19 litres
Contact: ktm.co.uk, 01280 709 500

GradeStudio

Check your answer

- Did you find a clear purpose?
- Did you find a clear audience?
- Did you find any other purposes?
- Did you find any other audiences?
- Did you find a detail to support each point you made?

My learning ▶

This lesson will help you to:
- practise an exam-style question
- assess your answer by looking at other responses.

Assessment practice

Now you are going to have a go at an exam-style question. Attempt the activity in the time suggested and then complete the Peer/Self-assessment activity that follows.

Activity 1

Read the article below and then take 10 minutes to answer this question:

What are the purposes of and audiences for this text?

New toe job a woe job, Paula

By **VIKKI ORVICE**

PAULA RADCLIFFE has been forced to pull out of this year's London Marathon because of a broken toe.

The world record holder was aiming to win her fourth London title on April 26 but suffered the injury on Tuesday while altitude training in New Mexico.

It comes exactly a year after she withdrew from last year's event with another toe problem.

That was the start of an injury-plagued year which resulted in her finishing only 23rd at the Beijing Olympics.

Radcliffe, who came back after Beijing to win the New York Marathon in style, intended to use London as a warm-up ahead of this summer's World Championships.

Her appearance on the start-line in Berlin could now be in jeopardy if she fails to recover in time.

Radcliffe, 35, set her world record in London in 2003 but has not competed there for four years.

She said: 'I am desperately disappointed that I have to pull out of this year's race.

'I was looking forward to running in front of the amazing crowds.

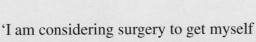

Sun

'I am considering surgery to get myself totally healthy as soon as physically possible and ultimately prevent any future problems.' London Marathon race director Dave Bedford said: 'This is a major blow for Paula. I know how much she wanted to run here this year but luck just does not seem to be on her side. 'Paula's priority must now be to get fully fit for the World Championships and we wish her all the best for a speedy recovery.' Meanwhile coach Charles Van Commenee, who took charge of British athletics last month, has targeted at least **FIVE** medals from the European Indoors in Turin starting today.

He said: 'We have a good history in this event, especially two years ago – when we won 10 medals with the home advantage in Birmingham.

'It would really be a disappointment if we end up with less.'

Peer/Self-assessment activity

1 Check your answer to Activity 1.
- Did you find more than one purpose?
- Did you find more than one audience?
- Did you support each point you made?

2 Now grade your answer to Activity 1 using the mark scheme below. You will need to be careful and precise in your marking. Before you do this, you might like to read some sample answers to this activity on pages 18 and 19.

D
- ▶ attempts to engage with activity
- ▶ identifies one or more points about purpose
- ▶ identifies one or more points about audience
- ▶ some evidence of supporting detail.

C
- ▶ clear attempt to engage with activity
- ▶ several different points about purpose supported
- ▶ several different points about audience supported.

B
- ▶ clear and effective engagement with task
- ▶ range of relevant points about purpose and audience supported
- ▶ clear understanding of purpose and audience.

GradeStudio

Here are three student answers to the activity on page 16.
What are the purposes of and audiences for this text?
Read the answers together with the examiner comments. Then check what you have learnt and try putting it into practice.

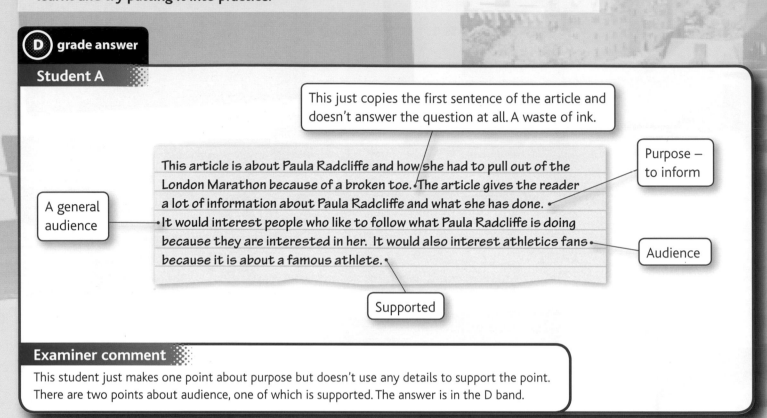

This just copies the first sentence of the article and doesn't answer the question at all. A waste of ink.

A general audience

Purpose – to inform

This article is about Paula Radcliffe and how she had to pull out of the London Marathon because of a broken toe. The article gives the reader a lot of information about Paula Radcliffe and what she has done. It would interest people who like to follow what Paula Radcliffe is doing because they are interested in her. It would also interest athletics fans because it is about a famous athlete.

Audience

Supported

Examiner comment

This student just makes one point about purpose but doesn't use any details to support the point. There are two points about audience, one of which is supported. The answer is in the D band.

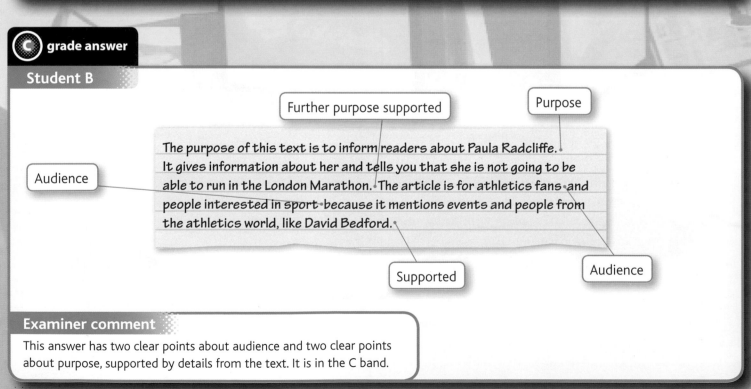

Further purpose supported

Purpose

Audience

The purpose of this text is to inform readers about Paula Radcliffe. It gives information about her and tells you that she is not going to be able to run in the London Marathon. The article is for athletics fans and people interested in sport because it mentions events and people from the athletics world, like David Bedford.

Supported

Audience

Examiner comment

This answer has two clear points about audience and two clear points about purpose, supported by details from the text. It is in the C band.

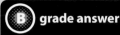

B grade answer

Student C

Supported

Audience

Supported

Audience

Audience

> This article appeals to sports fans because it is about a famous athlete, Paula Radcliffe. In particular it appeals to athletics fans because it tells us about her athletic achievements and, of course to fans of Paula Radcliffe because it is about her. Its purpose is to inform about what is happening to Paula now (her broken toe) and what has happened to her in the past (winning the New York Marathon).

Supported

Supported

Purpose

Purpose

Supported

Examiner comment

This is a detailed and efficient answer which contains three specific audiences and two clear purposes, each of them supported by a detail from the text. It is in the B band.

Purpose and audience

To move up the grades, you need to make a wider range of points and you need to support each of them with a detail from the text. You also need to make sure that you answer all parts of the question. Here, for example, you need to make sure that you make several points both about purpose and about audience. Student B did all three things – purpose, audience and supporting detail – but Student A didn't.

What have I learnt?

Discuss or jot down what you now know about:
- finding points to make about purpose
- finding points to make about audience
- answering the question
- finding precise support for the points you make
- what makes the difference between a D, C and B answer on purpose and audience.

Putting it into practice

- You can practise finding purpose and audience with any text you come across.
- Use any newspapers, magazines, pages from textbooks, letters and adverts.
- Practise finding precise detail to support the points you make.
- Give yourself about 10 minutes to practise this skill.

My learning ▶

This lesson will help you to:
- find the main points in an argument
- select material to answer the question.

Introducing arguments, facts and opinions

The use of facts and opinions is one of a writer's main tools in developing an argument.

What are arguments?

An **argument** is what the text has to say. There may be one or more main points.

When you are looking for arguments:

▶ always look at the headline first – there may be a clue

▶ try to work out what the main point of the article is

▶ recognise different stages in the argument as you read through.

What are facts?

A **fact** is something that can be proved. The most obvious facts are names and places and dates and figures because these can be looked up and checked. For example, the following statements are both facts.

▶ Rome is the capital of Italy.

▶ England won the football world cup in 1966.

When you are trying to find facts:

▶ don't read the whole article first – skim it

▶ look for names of places or people (with upper case letters) first

▶ then look for numbers or dates.

What are opinions?

An **opinion** is something that someone thinks, but is not necessarily true. For example, it is an opinion to claim that the Premier League is the best football league in the world.

When you are trying to find opinions:

▶ don't read the whole article first – skim it

▶ look for quotations (in quotation marks) first

▶ then when you read the article you can find other opinions – especially those of the writer.

The following annotated text gives you examples of facts, opinions and argument.

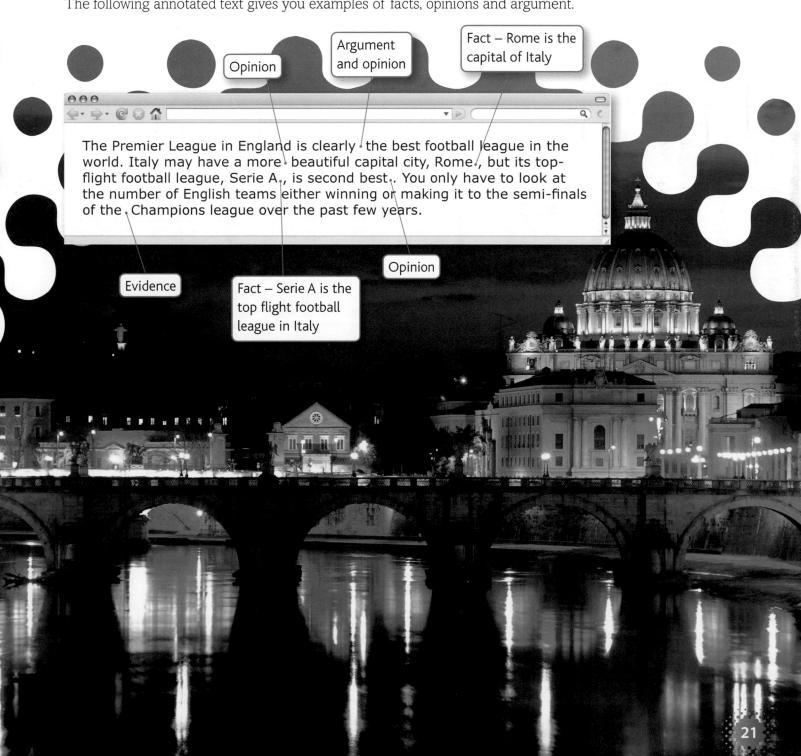

Opinion

Argument and opinion

Fact – Rome is the capital of Italy

The Premier League in England is clearly the best football league in the world. Italy may have a more beautiful capital city, Rome, but its top-flight football league, Serie A, is second best. You only have to look at the number of English teams either winning or making it to the semi-finals of the Champions league over the past few years.

Opinion

Evidence

Fact – Serie A is the top flight football league in Italy

Looking for facts, opinions and arguments

Activity 1 below asks you to find the material that the writer uses to support her argument. So you need to look for a range of different points that she makes and you need to think about some of the methods she uses. Does she use facts and opinions, for example? If so, where do the facts and opinions come from? Are they from different people and sources?

1 Read the article below, which was written about Jade Goody shortly before she died in 2009, and then discuss or make notes on the following.

   a What are the different reasons why Carole Malone thinks it is 'time to turn the cameras off'?

   b What aspects of Jade does she refer to?

   c What opinions of different people does she include?

   d How does she use her own experience?

2 Now answer the following question in full sentences:

How does Carole Malone support her argument that it is time to turn the cameras off Jade?

Time to turn the cameras off Jade

Is it just me who's starting to feel like the spectre at the feast? Am I the only one feeling grubby, ashamed and just a little bit sickened at watching a young woman die in front of my eyes?

Am I the only person looking at pictures of Jade Goody where her face is contorted with pain, when she's gasping for breath through an oxygen mask, where she stares through car windows with sad, dead eyes – and thinking **ENOUGH!**

Jade Goody has always been upfront about her reasons for allowing the cameras to film the various stages of her illness. She was always clear she was doing it so her sons would have enough money for the kind of life she never had. But that was before she knew she was going to die.

That was when she still knew her own mind.

Coping

And I was part of that deal. I interviewed her – twice. And I was proud of what we did. I was proud of how, together, we got what she wanted to say across to people who, till then, were suspicious about her motives for living and coping with this disease so publicly.

But when I spent time with Jade she could still talk. She could still think for

herself. She still had hope. She was still in control of what was happening to her.

And even when the doctors delivered her death sentence – on one of the very days I was interviewing her – even then she still had the strength to organise the wedding she had always dreamed of.

Back then – and incredibly it was only three weeks ago – Jade was in control of everything down to the caterers she wanted, the dress she wanted, her bridesmaids. She even set about organising a helicopter to take her to the ceremony.

But now she's not in control. Now, what's left of her life revolves around numbing the pain which often has her

screaming in agony. And when she's not begging doctors to get her out of the pain, she's flailing around in a drug-induced stupor – not knowing where she is or what she's doing.

And we're all watching that. We're all part of this gruesome peep show that's charting this young woman's final, agonising days. We're all staring wide-eyed through a window **SHE** opened not wanting to look – but not being able to resist.

Max Clifford said last week: 'Jade will tell us when she's had enough.'

Will she? How will she do that when she's slurring, semi-conscious and up to her eyeballs on morphine?

How's she going to tell the photographers waiting outside the hospital to go away when she needs every ounce of strength just to breathe and stay alive? How's she going to make them understand that being photographed in her nightie looking sick and distressed isn't how she wants people to see her?

And **I KNOW** she doesn't want people seeing her like that because when, just over a month ago, we took photos after she first lost her hair she was insistent on wearing beautiful clothes and having her make-up done.

'I might have cancer but I don't want to look like I have,' she told me. 'I still want to look pretty.'

But she doesn't look pretty any more. She looks sick. But most of all she looks

hunted – like an animal.

And it's frightening. Not just for all those people who presently have cancer who look at Jade and know what their end is going to be like. But it's terrifying for the rest of us who, for now at least, don't have cancer but see Jade as a hellish glimpse of what might be waiting for us down the years.

Macabre

The wedding should have been the cut-off point. Those photos of her in her wedding dress looking serene and beautiful – **THAT'S** the moment we should have bid Jade a dignified farewell.

THAT'S how we should have remembered her – happy, smiling, looking into the eyes of the man she adores and holding hands with the sons she will never see grow up.

Because what we're seeing now is macabre and dark. And it's gratuitous. I don't want to see Jade's last breath. I don't want to see her struggling to stay alive so her sons can be christened. I don't want to see her straining to give a thumbs-up sign to the cameras to make **US** feel better.

This is now a horror show – the only difference is that it's real.

Jade has lived her whole adult life in front of the cameras. But it's time now to turn them off. We've seen enough. She's shared enough.

Her final days belong to her – not us.

My learning ▶

This lesson will help you to:
- follow an argument
- understand how facts and opinions are used.

Arguments and writers' methods

The activity below is in two parts. The first part asks you to identify the argument so, when you are reading through the text, jot down the main points that are being made. Then it asks you how the writer supports the argument. To do this you will need to think about what he refers to, how he uses facts, how he uses opinions and whether these are from the same source or from different sources.

Activity 1

Read the text below. As you are reading, jot down the main points. Each time you do this, think about what method the writer is using.

Now answer the following question:

What is the writer's argument in this text and how does he support it?

THE INDEPENDENT

Hip-hop offers a new message

The aggressive image hides an intelligent aspect, says **Ian Burrell**

Not all hip-hop icons die young.

Grandmaster Flash, who turned 50 in January, dropped into Britain over Easter to rotate some turntables alongside the veteran spinner, Jazzy Jeff, 43. And last month, Big Daddy Kane, the epitome of the gold-chain wearing Eighties rapper, exercised his forty-something larynx in the classy environs of London's Jazz Café. Not everyone goes out in a hail of bullets like Tupac and Biggie.

That doesn't mean this is a music genre that has finally been allowed to come in from the street corner. More than ever it is derided as the voice of a crude braggadocio that incites violence and misogyny. Rap has a terrible rep. But it doesn't have to be like that, as Q-Tip, one of the finest rappers, recently demonstrated. The former member of Nineties rap act A Tribe Called Quest departed London's Roundhouse stage singing 'Life is Better', an unlikely sentiment from a genre often derided for its negativity. The lyric, the title of a track made with folk singer Norah Jones, was all the more powerful for Q-Tip having earlier climbed a barrier and entered the crowd, urging them to sing those words back to him.

There has always been a smart side to hip-hop, from Philadelphia's The Roots and New York's De La Soul, through to Nineties acts such as Slum Village, and more recently Lupe Fiasco and The Cool Kids. In Britain we have the likes of Sway and Akala, who is quick to alert his peers to the delights of Shakespeare. It's not a theme that has much interested politicians alarmed by drug-related violence, and looking to find something to blame. You can see why. When stabbings take place at the Urban Music Awards in London, as last November, hip-hop is hurt, though the incident was not specific to that music.

Without wishing to take the edge off a genre that has a tradition of challenging authority, I suggest that it won't be so long before hip-hop stakes a claim for a place in the schedules of BBC Radio 2. The lasting qualities of the music are beyond question and there is much on offer here for thinking people.

GradeStudio

Check your answer

- Did you use the title to help you?
- Did you find the main points?
- Did you mention facts which supported the argument?
- Did you mention the writer's use of opinions to support his argument?

Activity 2 below doesn't ask you about the argument itself. The question tells you what the main argument is. Instead it focuses just on the methods that are being used.

1 Read the article and question 2 below. As you read through the article, each time that you find a main point note down what method the writer has used. Is it:

- a reference
- a fact
- an opinion?

2 Now answer the following question:

How does the writer support the argument set out in the title of this article?

THE TIMES

News

Why a third wet summer would spell disaster for birds and bees

Kaya Burgess

Poor conditions could cause wildlife washout

Erratic weather and rainy summers are threatening many species of British wildlife, which are struggling to cope with the unseasonable conditions.

Insects such as butterflies and bees – as well as the birds that feed on them – were all hit by the second consecutive summer of 'foul and abusive' weather, and could be in danger if there is a third, the National Trust has warned.

Matthew Oates, the Trust's conservation adviser, said: 'A cold, late spring, a wet summer with few sunny days and the long dry autumn has shown how dependent our wildlife is on the climate.

'Many iconic species closely associated with the four seasons are having to cope with higher incidences of poor weather as our climate becomes more unpredictable.'

Many species were confused by last year's warm winter, which caused them to flit 'in and out of hibernation mode' – a problem that could recur if temperatures rise in the new year as drastically as predicted.

'After two very poor years in a row we desperately need a good summer in 2009 – otherwise it's going to look increasingly grim for a wealth of wildlife in the UK,' Mr Oates added.

Colonies of bees are collapsing in the washout weather, and many birds are struggling to feed their young as a result. Gale-force winds have also reduced the butterfly population.

Blue and great tits suffered from a lack of insects and bad weather in May, and coastal birds, such as choughs, kittiwakes and razorbills, bred late and had few young. In July nightjars raised only one youngster on average, and puffin numbers on the Farne Islands, off Northumberland, were down by a third over five years.

In late summer wasps were conspicuous by their low numbers. Other insects affected included the common autumn crane fly and the small tortoiseshell butterfly. Cabbage white butterflies were unusually plentiful.

Of the few plants flourishing in the wet weather, many are harmful such as ragwort, a weed poisonous to horses, which has sprung up in the newly drenched spaces left by droughts in 2006. Many trees have been struggling to put out berries after the bitterly cold spring this year.

Mr Oates said: 'There's no such thing as a normal year, but there do seem to be more extreme, adverse events at inappropriate times of the year.' He said that a third year of bad weather could do 'immense damage' and lead to certain flora and fauna dying out in some areas.

Otters are desperate too. One swam two miles out to the Farne Islands

Under the weather

- Great and blue tits were among birds whose nests failed due to lack of insects and foul weather in May
- Insects including butterflies, moths, hoverflies, ladybirds and dragonflies all had a poor summer
- Puffin numbers on the Farne Islands are down by 35 per cent in five years, according to data collected in July
- The common crane fly, usually so abundant as to be a pest, showed a 'remarkable and perhaps unprecedented' scarcity
- An otter made the two-mile sea crossing to the Farne Islands for the first time on record despite stormy weather in November
- Many lesser horse-shoe bats were underweight due to the scarcity of insects

GradeStudio

Check your answer

- Did you find several different points?
- Did you mention the facts used?
- Did you mention the opinions used?

This lesson will help you to:
- practise an exam-style question
- assess your answer by looking at other responses.

Assessment practice

Now you are going to have a go at an exam-style question. Attempt the activity in the time suggested and then complete the Peer/Self-assessment activity that follows.

This activity is asking you to distinguish between the Rose Report and what the newspaper says about the report. The question is about the newspaper's view so you don't need to include what the report itself says.

Also, you are not being asked about methods in this activity. You are just being asked to find the different points that are made to show the newspaper's view of the report.

List each point that the newspaper makes where it is showing its own view.

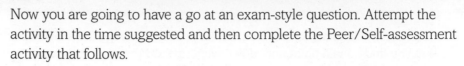

Activity 1

1 Read through the newspaper article opposite. This article, from *The Independent*, is about the Rose Report on primary school education. In the exam, rather than listing each point, you can underline them on the exam paper.

2 Now answer the following question:

What is *The Independent*'s view about the Rose Report?

Let schools decide how to teach

Sir Jim Rose's review of primary school teaching, commissioned by the Government, has been touted as a blueprint for the most radical reform of education in two decades. The interim report certainly contains suggestions that will have traditionalists spluttering with indignation.

Sir Jim argues that 'areas of learning' should replace individual 'non-core' subjects such as history, geography and science. He also recommends that 'emotional well-being' and 'social skills' should be a compulsory part of the curriculum. Another suggestion is that computer skills should be taught to primary school children, rather than introducing such tuition at secondary school level as at present. Already, the report has been accused of advocating further dumbing down of our education system. Others have criticised it for asking teachers to do the job of parents by teaching children how to behave and interact with others.

Yet these objections rather miss the point. Many primary schools already blur traditional subject boundaries in class. They have made a choice about the most effective way to impart knowledge

THE INDEPENDENT

and understanding. This is the real issue. The goal of primary education reform should be to let individual schools tailor lessons as they see fit. If schools want to conduct lessons in history, or the vaguer 'human, social and environmental understanding', that should be a matter for them.

As for imparting social skills, again, let individual schools tailor their approach according to their intake. Let them make a judgement on what is likely to produce the best educational results. The Rose Report suggests that children should be taught to use podcasts or make their own radio programmes. But that might not be appropriate in many schools where the priority will, rightly, be on raising basic literacy levels. The point is to let the individual schools and teachers decide the best way to teach.

At present there are too many tests and the curriculum is over-loaded. Schools need to be given the power to ignore top-down directives. If this report can help set primary schools free, it might well live up to its billing as the most significant shake-up in primary education in 20 years. Otherwise, it will end up as just the latest in a long line of meddling and counter-productive prescriptions from Whitehall.

Peer/Self-assessment activity

1 Check your answer to Activity 1. Did you manage to:
   • find several different points
   • present these clearly
   • make everything you wrote relevant to the question
   • avoid repeating the same point?

2 Now grade your answer to Activity 1 using the mark scheme below. You will need to be careful and precise in your marking. Before you do this, you might like to read some sample answers to this activity on pages 28 and 29.

D
▶ identifies two or more main points
▶ most of the writing focused on the newspaper's views
▶ some attempt to find material directly relevant to the activity.

C
▶ clear attempt to engage with the activity
▶ several different points made
▶ some understanding of the newspaper's view.

B
▶ clear and effective engagement with activity
▶ range of relevant points made
▶ clear understanding of the newspaper's view.

GradeStudio

Here are three student answers to the activity on page 26.
What is The Independent*'s view about the Rose Report?*
Read the answers together with the examiner comments. Then check what you have learnt and try putting it into practice.

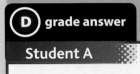 **grade answer**

Student A

Accurate information about the report but not tied to question

Ditto

This is the report's view, not *The Independent*'s

Another point the newspaper agrees with

The Rose Report has been described as a very radical one. It recommends that individual subjects should be replaced by 'areas of learning'. It recommends that computer skills should be taught. Schools should decide for themselves what they should teach. There are too many tests at the moment and there are too many subjects.

This is a view the paper agrees with

Not quite what is said

Examiner comment

The first part of the answer says what the Rose Report says, not what the newspaper thinks. The student needs to use the key words of the activity in order to make the points completely relevant. Three points are made (two of them clearly) in the last two sentences. The answer is in the D band.

 **grade answer**

Student B

Clear point

Newspaper's view

The report says that the Rose Report will upset traditionalists. The newspaper thinks that it is right for primary schools to choose how to teach. It thinks that the idea of children making their own podcasts is silly. It also thinks there are too many tests at the moment.

Clear point

Clear point

Examiner comment

This answer selects four clear points which the newspaper makes in order to make its views known. It is a clear answer, has several different points and shows some understanding of the newspaper's view. It is in the C band.

B grade answer

Student C

Clear point   Clear point   Clear point

Clear point

The newspaper realises that the Rose Report will upset traditionalists.
It agrees that schools should decide what to teach and how. This should
be appropriate to the children in the school. The report makes too many
specific suggestions . The newspaper thinks there are too many tests
and that schools should ignore government interference in order to be
free and effective.

Clear point

Developed answer

Clear point

Clear point

Examiner comment

This is a full, clear and detailed answer which covers all the main points about the newspaper's views. It uses the key words of the activity in the answer and therefore makes sure that it keeps on track all the way through. It is in the B band.

Argument, fact and opinion

To move up the grades, read the question before you read the passage. When you are reading the text underline the key points so that when you have finished you just have to write the answer out. Don't copy out more than you need to. If you are showing the different points in an argument, make sure that you don't repeat yourself.

What have I learnt?

Discuss or jot down what you now know about:
- following an argument
- finding the main points in an argument
- answering the question
- finding facts which support the argument
- finding opinions which support the argument.

Putting it into practice

- You can practise this skill with any text you come across.
- Work out what is the main point being made.
- Find the different points that make up the argument.
- Take a few minutes to find some facts.
- Take a few minutes to find some opinions.

My learning ▶

This lesson will help you to:
- read between the lines
- select material to answer questions about implications and assumptions.

Introducing implications and assumptions

What are implications?

An **implication** is something that is suggested but not directly said. For example, when the boxer Mohammed Ali described himself as being able to 'Float like a butterfly and sting like a bee' he was implying that he could move quickly on his feet and could punch very hard.

What are assumptions?

An **assumption** is something that you are expected to know and as a result it isn't explained. Or it could be something about the reader that the writer has taken for granted. This can be useful when you are trying to work out the audience of a piece of text.

For example, if a text says that hearing aids are being sold at a discount to people aged over 60, then the assumption is that the readers will be over 60 or will know someone over 60.

If a holiday is advertised with a special deal of four weeks for the price of three, then it is assumed that its readers are people with four weeks spare to go on holiday.

GradeStudio

Examiner tips

In the exam you will be asked to:
- work out what is being hinted at in a text
- think about what the writer assumes the reader knows
- think about what the writer assumes the reader doesn't know
- answer questions about implications and assumptions.

Activity 1

A lot of what we read in newspapers and magazines is designed for people with special interests. Those without these interests will simply ignore such material.

Look at the three short texts below and opposite.

What assumptions are they making about who will read these texts and what their interests are?

Tourist Rates

	Bank sells	Bank buys
Australia Dollars	1.79	2.14
Barbados Dollars	2.89	3.43
Brazil Real	2.51	3.02
Canada Dollars	1.42	1.92
Denmark Kroner	8.26	9.28
Egypt Pounds	8.07	9.71

YOUR HOROSCOPE

Taurus
April 21 – May 21

YOU may be put off by someone who seems to know more than you, or are they just showing off? Maybe they are playing the big 'I am' to get your attention – which begs the question, why? From love to work you're being sought out.

Daily Mirror

WORLD OF SPORT

Perfect Rossi

MOTOGP

VALENTINO ROSSI doubled his lead in the World MotoGP title chase with a runaway win in the Czech Republic.

Rossi scored his fifth victory of the campaign to go 50 points clear in the 11th round at Brno, where nearest rival, Fiat Yamaha team-mate Jorge Lorenzo, crashed.

'That was a great race, nearly perfect,' said Rossi, who finished some 12 seconds ahead of Repsol Honda's Dani Pedrosa. Toni Elias was third while Yorkshireman James Toseland ended up ninth.

DAVE FERN

Daily Express

Activity 2 asks you to look for things that are assumed about the audience of the text. The text is a 'leader' article from a newspaper. A leader is printed on the editorial page and gives the view of the newspaper on a topical issue. This one discusses a television programme and financial problems in the government's Treasury department.

Activity 2

Read the text below and then complete the short answer questions and finally answer the full question.

The short answer questions will help prepare you to write the full answer by taking you through the different stages.

1 Discuss or write down answers to the following questions.

   a What TV programme does it expect the reader to know about?

   b Which people are the readers supposed to recognise?

   c What one piece of information is given about Rachel Riley, and why?

   d What political point is the leader making?

   For each answer give a detail from the text to support your idea.

2 Now answer the following question:

   What assumptions does the leader make about its readers, and what is the article really about?

NEWS OF THE WORLD

We've got it figured

REPORTS that *Countdown*'s Rachel Riley's maths aren't up to predecessor Carol Vorderman's standard may not equal disaster.

After all, if Oxford graduate Rachel fails her sums on the Channel 4 show she can always try the Treasury.

<u>*Where the numbers seldom add up.*</u>

GradeStudio

Examiner tips

- When you are asked to 'give a detail from the text to support your idea' you need to find a short part of the text which supports the point that you are making. For instance, if you made the point that this article refers to a television programme, then 'Countdown' would be the detail of the text which supported your point.

- The examiner wants to know what bits of text you are looking at so always include one detail from the text to support the point that you are making.

GradeStudio

Check your answer

- Did you answer all of the short answer questions in part 1?
- Did you answer each of the two questions in part 2?
- Did you answer the two main questions in the order they appeared?
- Did you give a piece of evidence from the text to support each point you made?

This lesson will help you to:
- think about the implications of what is written
- think about the assumptions that the writer makes about the readers.

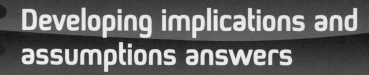

Developing implications and assumptions answers

When you are reading a text ask yourself some of these questions.

▶ What am I meant to know?

▶ If I don't understand it, what is the writer assuming I know?

▶ What is spelt out for me and what is not?

When you are answering a question, use the key words of the activity all the way through your answer in order to make sure that you keep on track.

Activity 1

This activity asks you to think about assumptions and implications. Read the text below which is about cod liver oil. The following questions will help to identify some material first.

1 What does the text imply about other cod liver oil products?

2 What does it imply about the taste of 'normal' cod liver oil?

3 What does it imply about the effect of 'normal' cod liver oil?

4 What does it assume the reader knows about cod liver oil already?

5 What sorts of issues does it assume the reader cares about?

6 What kinds of readers is this advertisement aimed at?

For each point you make, identify a detail from the text which you could use to support your point.

Now answer the following question:

What assumptions does this text make about the kinds of people who might buy this product and how does it imply that this product is better than others?

GradeStudio

Check your answer

- Did you find the scientific material?
- Did you find the environmental material?
- Did you find how it tries to persuade you that this is better than 'normal' cod liver oil?
- Did you support each point by referring to a detail in the text?

We're very proud of the quality of our cod liver oil at Healthspan and with good reason. Independent tests on 33 cod liver oil products available in the UK showed that ours was the purest of all those tested.

We source our cod liver oil from the unpolluted, sustainable fisheries of Iceland and refine it further using advanced, filter-pure technology. It is then odour-neutralised to avoid the problems associated with repeating after swallowing. Our unique 'non-fishy' St Clement's cod liver oil liquid and capsules contain cold-pressed citrus oils for all the fish oil goodness without the 'yuk' factor. The active elements in cod liver oil are the omega 3 fatty acids that it contains. You should look for the amount of the two key omega 3 fatty acids – DHA and EPA – on any cod liver oil product. Ours contain particularly high levels so that you can be sure of all the health benefits with a regular daily capsule or spoonful.

SOURCED FROM SUSTAINABLE WATERS

The purest Icelandic
cod liver oil

Activity 2 asks you to look for three different but related things. It asks:

▶ very specific questions about assumptions

▶ what is implied about the article's attitude about one person

▶ what is implied about the royal family.

So there are three things to be thinking about while you are reading the text.

Read the text below and then answer the following questions:

1 What does the text assume the reader is interested in?

2 What is its attitude towards the Queen?

3 What does the overall article imply about the royal family?

Use a detail from the text to support each point you make.

Ve are not amused!

QUEEN: FILM VICTORIA IS TOO GERMAN

The Queen has seen a special screening of Fergie's film *The Young Victoria* – and complained it was too **GERMAN.**

Her Majesty *(descended from a long line of Germans)* was shown the movie about her great great gran Queen Victoria *(quite a lot German)* and Prince Albert *(all German)* at Buckingham Palace. While her ex daughter-in-law's production wasn't the wurst she'd seen, she found the German bits heil-y overdone.

A senior source said: 'She thought the film had a lot of good points but she is a stickler for accuracy. She wasn't too impressed they had Albert diving in front of Victoria to take the bullet in an assassination attempt.

By **ROBERT JOBSON,** ROYAL EDITOR

'It simply did not happen and Her Majesty questioned the need for such a dramatic inaccuracy. She also thought the uniforms worn by the British officers looked too Germanic.'

Prince Andrew's ex Sarah Ferguson produced *The Young Victoria* after becoming fascinated with the legendary Queen's life.

Her daughter Beatrice has a cameo role in the film, which is currently No 4 in the UK box office chart.

MOVIE GRAN:
Victoria

NEWS OF THE WORLD

GradeStudio

Check your answer

● Did you mention the obvious – the film and the royal family?

● Did you find any implications about the Queen and her views?

● Did you put the information about different members of the royal family together to come to any conclusions about what the article suggested about them?

This lesson will help you to:
● practise an exam-style question
● assess your answer by looking at other responses.

Assessment practice

Now you are going to have a go at an exam-style question. Attempt the activity in the time suggested and then complete the Peer/Self-assessment activity that follows.

Activity 1

Read the text below and then take 10 minutes to answer the following question:

What assumptions does the writer make about what the reader is interested in and what does the article imply about football and some of its supporters?

Support your points by references to detail in the text.

LEAGUE ONE Score

LUCKY 13!
Steve strikes as fans hurl missiles

■ MORR THE MERRIER – Leicester defender Michael Morrison wins the ball against Millwall striker Gary Alexander

MILLWALL 0
LEICESTER 1

By **BILL PIERCE** at The Den

STEVE HOWARD'S 13th goal of the season put runaway leaders Leicester back on track for the title.

But furious Millwall players were convinced he should have been sent off for elbowing Lions skipper Tony Craig.

Howard struck powerfully from 25 yards after good work by Lloyd Dyer in the 21st minute.

But trouble flared when Millwall's notorious fans hurled missiles at linesman Phil Melin for not flagging for offside in the build-up.

Referee Tony Taylor handed an object to police.

Later, 150 Millwall fans threw missiles at police outside the ground and five people were arrested, with a police horse suffering minor injuries.

SPORT

Leicester boss Nigel Pearson and his staff came in for another bombardment during the game and the Lions seem certain to face an FA inquiry into the incidents.

The fans gave ref Taylor more stick when Craig was clattered by Howard 15 minutes after the goal.

Howard was only booked, but so was Millwall's Andy Frampton for racing up to the referee and miming a swinging elbow.

Pearson said: 'Most fans are great but, like everybody, I don't like these sort of things. It is up to the officials and authorities to sort it out.

Protests

'What disappointed me most was Steve's booking for the challenge.

'I've had a word with the ref and asked him whether he would have booked a player if there had not been such a response by the Millwall players and the fans.'

Lions boss Kenny Jackett refused to condemn Howard but said: 'I've every faith in Tony as a player and a man. He doesn't go down easily.

'Yes, Frampton was booked for his protests but sometimes our reputation goes before us.'

Millwall were a class below their visitors, who stay nine points clear at the top with eight games to go.

Matty Fryatt, Howard's 28-goal strike partner, went close to making it 2-0 with a shot against the foot of a post 11 minutes from time.

And another goal would not have flattered the Foxes.

NEWS OF THE WORLD

Peer/Self-assessment activity

1 Check your answer to Activity 1. Did you:
   - notice that the headline and the subheading were about different things
   - find how the feelings of the players were described
   - notice how the fans were described
   - notice the attitude of Kenny Jackett?

2 Now grade your answer to Activity 1 using the mark scheme below. You will need to be careful and precise in your marking. Before you do this, you might like to read some sample answers on this activity on pages 36 and 37.

D
- identifies two or more points
- most of the writing focused on the activity
- attempts to engage with activity.

C
- clear attempt to engage with activity
- several different points made
- some focus on implications about football and implications about fans.

B
- clear and effective engagement with activity
- range of relevant points made
- clear understanding of assumptions and implications.

GradeStudio

Here are three student answers to the activity on page 34.

What assumptions does the writer make about what the reader is interested in and what does the article imply about football and some of its supporters?

Read the answers together with the examiner comments. Then check what you have learnt and try putting it into practice.

D grade answer

Student A

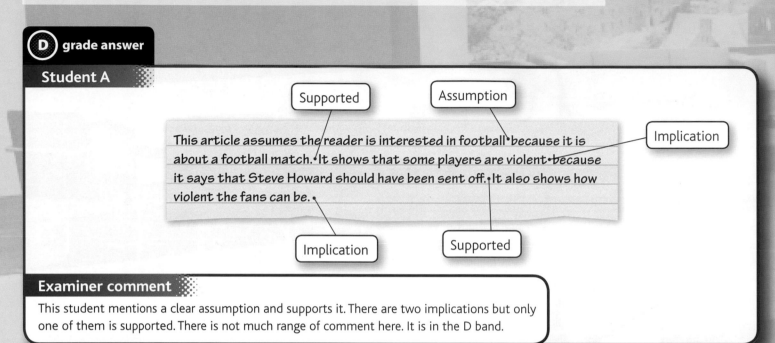

Supported

Assumption

Implication

This article assumes the reader is interested in football because it is about a football match. It shows that some players are violent because it says that Steve Howard should have been sent off. It also shows how violent the fans can be.

Implication

Supported

Examiner comment

This student mentions a clear assumption and supports it. There are two implications but only one of them is supported. There is not much range of comment here. It is in the D band.

C grade answer

Student B

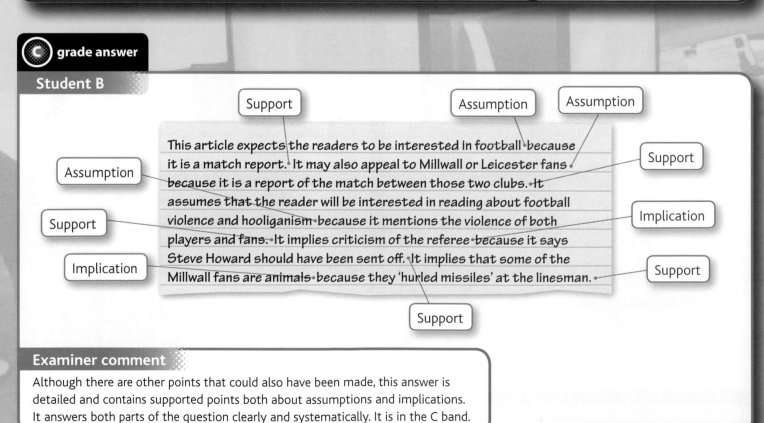

Support

Assumption

Assumption

Assumption

Support

Implication

This article expects the readers to be interested in football because it is a match report. It may also appeal to Millwall or Leicester fans because it is a report of the match between those two clubs. It assumes that the reader will be interested in reading about football violence and hooliganism because it mentions the violence of both players and fans. It implies criticism of the referee because it says Steve Howard should have been sent off. It implies that some of the Millwall fans are animals because they 'hurled missiles' at the linesman.

Support

Implication

Support

Support

Examiner comment

Although there are other points that could also have been made, this answer is detailed and contains supported points both about assumptions and implications. It answers both parts of the question clearly and systematically. It is in the C band.

B grade answer

Student C

Assumption

Assumption

The writer assumes that the reader is interested in the details of a football match, and also interested in stories about the behaviour of so-called fans. It may appeal to Millwall and Leicester fans because it is a report of a match between the two clubs.
The writer calls Millwall fans 'notorious' and exaggerates by saying that they hurled 'missiles' at the linesman and at the police, stereotyping them unfavourably. The article suggests that referees are too lenient because Howard was 'only booked'. It also suggests that the Leicester manager is biased for thinking punishments too lenient, and that the Millwall manager is biased for thinking the punishments too harsh.
Overall the report seems to suggest that football is a violent sport, supported by thugs.

More detailed assumption, supported

Implication about football and fans

Supported

Implication

Implication

Conclusion about attitudes

Implication

Examiner comment

This is a full and detailed answer which makes a wide range of points and supports them by reference to the text's details. It engages effectively with all three parts of the task and shows clear understanding of assumptions and implications. It is well into the B band.

 MOVING UP THE GRADES

Implications and assumptions

To move up the grades, you need to make a wide range of points and make sure that you answer all parts of the question if there is more than one part to it. This is clearly shown in the difference between Student A (who answers some of the question in detail) and Student B (who uses some detail and support) and Student C (who makes a range of points about both assumptions and implications, supporting them effectively and systematically). You can move up the grades by making sure that you support all your points and that the references to the text are specific.

What have I learnt?

Discuss or jot down what you now know about:

- finding assumptions in a text
- finding implications in a text
- supporting your points by reference to the text's details
- what makes the difference between a D, C and B answer.

Putting it into practice

- You can practise this skill with several of the texts you come across.
- Ask yourself what the text assumes the reader knows, what it doesn't assume the reader knows and what it implies about something rather than directly stating it.
- Give yourself 10 minutes to practise this skill.

My learning ▶

This lesson will help you to:
- identify and name language features
- comment on the effect of language features.

GradeStudio

Examiner tip

In the exam you are likely to be asked:
- to identify language and grammar features and comment on their effects.

Introducing language

You know a great deal about language because you have been studying it since you started school. In the exam, though, students often forget about some of the basic things they know about, such as:

▶ **nouns** (often names of things), e.g. *book, page*

▶ **verbs** (often doing words), e.g. *read, run*

▶ **adjectives** (words describing a noun), e.g. *bright, green*

▶ **adverbs** (words describing a verb), e.g. *quickly, slowly*.

There are many other things you know about, too, because you have come across them frequently, such as:

▶ **first person**, e.g. *I, we*

▶ **second person**, e.g. *you*

▶ **third person**, e.g. *he, she, it, they*

▶ **metaphor**, e.g. *the room is a prison*

▶ **simile**, e.g. *the room is like a prison*

▶ **alliteration**, e.g. *grimy green gunk*

▶ **repetition**, e.g. *location, location, location*

▶ **rhyme**, e.g. *soar, roar*

▶ **slang**, e.g. *bling*

▶ **puns**, e.g. *the footballer kitted his kitchen out.*

Some of you will have looked at some other language techniques, such as:

▶ **onomatopoeia** (where the sound of the word is like the sound of the thing), e.g. *click*

▶ **paradox** (where two apparently opposite things are both true), e.g. *a huge mouse*

▶ **assonance** (repetition of the same vowel sounds in different words), e.g. *how now brown cow*

▶ **jargon** (specialist language), e.g. *mouse, browser, link* all have special meanings when you are talking about computers.

However, you are only going to have time to write about a few of these in the time in the exam. What is important is that you can quickly identify a range of language features so that you can use some of them as the basis for commenting on their effect on the reader.

1 Look at the following article and identify as many language features as you can. Find an example of each of the following:

- alliteration
- military image
- slang
- cliché
- greyhound racing analogy
- words showing aggression
- snooker jargon
- metaphor
- hyperbole (exaggeration)
- house cleaning analogy.

2 For as many of the above features as you can, say what effect each has on the reader.

3 Now answer this question:

How does the writer use language to make the article dramatic and interesting?

You won't have time to include everything you have found, but see how many different points you can make. For each different language feature you name, use this method of answering:

The writer uses [name the language feature] [give the example of it from the text]
in order to make the reader [comment on the effect of the language feature].

Write as many of these sentences as you can.

Higgins and Murphy set up Crucible cracker

by DARREN LEWIS

It was nip and tuck all the way as John Higgins and Shaun Murphy fought out the first two sessions of the Betfred. com World Snooker Final last night.

With a cool £250,000 cheque for the winner it was little wonder that neither player was willing to give any quarter with the afternoon session finishing 4-4.

Higgins (inset) was fastest out of the traps, posting a 3-1 lead at The Crucible.

But 2005 winner Murphy hit back by taking the next four frames.

Higgins, bidding for his third world title, composed himself enough to level at 4-4 going into last night's evening session. And when they returned the Scot slipped a 57 break into the opening frame to move 5-4 ahead.

Murphy hit back immediately with a 52 to level and then looked set to retake the lead but his failure to get out of a devilishly worked snooker allowed Higgins to clean up for 6-5 lead.

And with Murphy failing to take the chances that he had hoovered up to get this far, Higgins took the next to go 7-5 up by the mid-session interval.

Daily Mirror

GradeStudio

Check your answer

Did you:

- manage to write at least five sentences
- include five different language features
- make a comment about the effect of each of them on the reader?

My learning ▶

This lesson will help you to:
- identify grammar features and comment on their effects
- identify language features and comment on their effects.

Introducing grammar and practising language and grammar questions

In the exam you might be asked to comment on grammar. Grammar is the construction which makes the sentence hang together properly. There are four basic kinds of sentence which are frequently used:

▶ **Simple sentence**

This is a sentence (usually a short one) with a subject and a main verb. For example:

I went shopping.

▶ **Compound sentence**

This is a series of two or more simple sentences joined together (usually with 'and' or 'but'). For example:

I went shopping and bought Bill a birthday present but I then decided to have lunch.

▶ **Complex sentence**

This is a longer sentence with one part dependent upon another (using what is called a subordinating conjunction such as 'although', because', 'until'). For example:

subordinating conjunction

I went shopping because I needed to buy Bill a birthday present.

▶ **Minor sentence**

This is a sentence which breaks the rules of grammar because it doesn't have a verb in it! These are often used for dramatic effect, to provide contrast to what has gone before or to jolt the reader. For example:

Gutted!

You can also identify and comment on particular kinds of sentences, such as questions, exclamations, rhetorical questions and any sentences that have unconventional grammar which breaks the rules or a deliberate grammatical mistake. Common examples of this are starting a sentence with a conjunction like 'and' or 'but' in order to sound informal or to show that rules can be broken.

A good way to answer the kind of question in Activity 1 below is to:

▶ identify and label what features you can find

▶ take each in turn

▶ name the feature

▶ give the example

▶ make a comment (in this text, which is about ugly cars, it is about how the writer pokes fun).

Do this for as many different features as you can.

Activity 1

Read the article below, taken from the Internet, and then answer the following question:

How does this article use language and grammar features to poke fun at the Toyota Scion XB?

The definitive guide to the ugliest cars ever

Toyota Scion XB

This giant yellow Lego brick on wheels would leave members of the public in stitches after seeing it on their way to the shops, so it's probably a good thing this US exclusive vehicle has never made it over into the UK.

Scrape off the yellow paintwork, and give it police colours, and you could use it as a battering ram to get through the front doors of criminals' houses, or a stage prop for the latest Rihanna concert. But as a car for getting from A to B, the Scion seriously sucks.

It's a rare error from Toyota, and certainly a memorable one. But we forgive the Japanese giant for giving us the environmentally-friendly Prius and cool inner city car known as the iQ.

GradeStudio

Check your answer

● Did you deal with more than one language feature?

● Did you deal with more than one grammar feature?

● Did you make a comment about each of them?

From Orange website

This lesson will help you to:
- practise exam-style questions
- assess your answer by looking at other responses.

Assessment practice

In the exam you might be asked to comment on the effect of language and grammar choices in any text. Activity 1 below uses a different kind of text, describing nature.

Activity 1

Read the text below to identify some features of language and grammar and then spend 10 minutes answering the following question:

How does the writer use language and grammar to bring this country scene to life?

The Walnut Tree

The immense, solitary, half-veiled autumn land is hissing with the kisses of rain in elms and hedgerows and grass, and underfoot the tunnelled soil gurgles and croaks. Secret and content, as if enjoying a blessed interval of life, are the small reedy pools where the moorhens hoot and nod in the grey water; beautiful the hundred pewits rising in ordered flight as they bereave the grey field and, wheeling over the leagues that seem all their own, presently make another field all a-flower by their alighting; almost happy once more is the tall, weedy mill by the broken water-gates, dying because no man inhabits it, its smooth wooden wheels and shoots and pillars fair and clean still under the red roof, though the wall is half fallen.

And in the heart of this, set in the dense rain, is a farmhouse far from any road; and round it the fields meet with many angles, and the hedges wind to make way, here, for a pond, deep underneath alders; there, for some scattered parcels of hayricks, on a grassy plot, encircling a large walnut tree; and for another pond, beside an apple orchard, whose trunks are lean and old and bent like the ribs of a wreck. A quadrangle of stalls, red tiled, or grey timber – trampled straw in their midst – adjoins the house, which is a red-grey cube, white windowed, with tall, stout chimneys and steep, auburn roof, and green stonecrop frothing over its porch. In and out goes a rutted, grassy track, lined by decapitated and still-living remains of many ancient elms.

In the overhanging elm branches flicker the straws of the long-past harvest, and the spirits of summers and autumns long past cling to grass and ponds and trees.

GradeStudio

Check your answer

Did you:
- comment on the effect of several language features
- comment on the effect of several grammar features?

Now you are going to have a go at another exam-style question. Attempt Activity 2 in the time suggested and then complete the Peer/Self-assessment activity that follows.

Activity 2

Read the article below and then spend 15 minutes answering this question:

How does the writer use language and grammar to entertain the reader?

METRO

The fantastic Mr Fly

BY ROSS McGUINNESS

A NEW musical talent has spread his wings and is already generating quite a bit of a buzz.

Meet Mr Fly, a piano-playing, guitar-bashing, musical genius from the insect world.

When he's not on stage or throwing up over his own food, he enjoys skateboarding, cycling and flying his kite.

Multi-talented: Mr Fly shows off in a skate park before tinkling the ivories (below).

Mr Fly is the unlikely muse of Belgian amateur photographer Nicholas Hendrickx.

Like his near namesake Jimi, the 21-year-old has torn up the rule book in his chosen field.

Nearly all the photographs of Mr Fly, whose first name is Gerald, were taken in Mr Hendrickx's bedroom, using mostly natural light and a small eight megapixel camera.

'I met Gerald Fly in my garden as I was shooting some flowers,' Mr Hendrickx said. 'There he was, staring at me with his big mosaic eyes, begging me for help. I offered him a job as my new model. That night we had a good drink and talked about potential photo shoots.'

'Surprisingly, he proved himself a lovely pianist and guitar player.'

In reality, Gerald is one of a number of flies which Mr Hendrickx photographs using props. 'It took quite some time. Some flies were great to work with, while others were very frustrating.'

'I guess it's normal – flies and humans aren't made to work together. Flies are made to annoy us with their buzzing and pooping on stuff.' In explaining why he chose to put flies in front of the camera, Mr Hendrickx said: 'I guess I just wanted people to enjoy the little things in life and to give them a refreshing view on insect macro-photography.' He insists most of the shots feature live specimens, but how he gets a bug to read the paper on a deckchair is anyone's guess.

As for Gerald, he is reportedly seeking fame with his band The Buzzes, winging it through (very) small venues throughout Europe.

Peer/Self-assessment activity

1 Check your answer to Activity 2. Did you:
   • find several language features
   • find several grammar features
   • comment on the effect of each of them?

2 Now grade your answer to Activity 2 using the mark scheme below. Before you do this you might like to read some sample answers on this task on pages 44 and 45.

D
▸ identifies two or more features
▸ comments on both language and grammar features
▸ some extra material.

C
▸ clear attempt to engage with activity
▸ range of relevant points
▸ both language and grammar features covered
▸ comments on both language and grammar features.

B
▸ clear attempt to engage with activity
▸ range of relevant points
▸ both language and grammar features well covered
▸ thoughtful comments on both language and grammar features.

GradeStudio

Here are two student answers to the activity on page 43.

How does the writer use language and grammar to entertain the reader?

Read the answers together with the examiner comments. Then check what you have learnt and try putting it into practice.

B grade answer

Student A

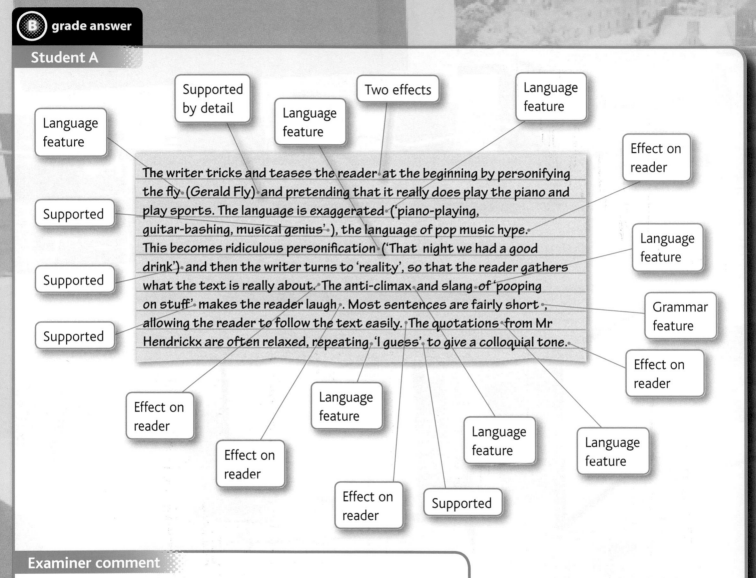

Supported by detail

Two effects

Language feature

Language feature

Language feature

Effect on reader

Supported

Language feature

Supported

Grammar feature

Supported

Effect on reader

Effect on reader

Language feature

Effect on reader

Language feature

Language feature

Effect on reader

Supported

The writer tricks and teases the reader at the beginning by personifying the fly (Gerald Fly) and pretending that it really does play the piano and play sports. The language is exaggerated ('piano-playing, guitar-bashing, musical genius'), the language of pop music hype. This becomes ridiculous personification ('That night we had a good drink') and then the writer turns to 'reality', so that the reader gathers what the text is really about. The anti-climax and slang of 'pooping on stuff' makes the reader laugh. Most sentences are fairly short, allowing the reader to follow the text easily. The quotations from Mr Hendrickx are often relaxed, repeating 'I guess' to give a colloquial tone.

Examiner comment

This full and detailed answer makes a range of points about both language and grammar features and keeps tying them to the effect. It is succinctly written and packed with points, supporting detail and effects. It is well into the B band.

D grade answer

Student B

Language feature

Not relevant to task

Not relevant to task and
not really true either

Another language
feature but no
comment on effect

> This article is about a fly that does amazing things. It plays the piano
> and the guitar and plays various different sports. The writer uses
> personification by giving the fly a name, Gerald Fly, and this amuses the
> reader. He also uses slang ('winging it') which is also a pun. Most of the
> sentences are the same length. This is to make it easy to read.

Comment
on effect

Very general
grammar feature

Supported

Supported

Simple comment on
effect but not supported

Examiner comment

The first two sentences aren't answering the question. Three language features are
identified and there is some support by use of details from the text, but there is
only one clear comment on effect. An attempt is made to comment on grammar,
but only one very general point is made. The answer falls into the D band.

Language and grammar features

To move up the grades, make sure you identify
features in the activity before you read the text.
Then for each feature that you mention:

- name the feature
- give an example
- make a comment.

This will keep you on track throughout your answer
and the more of these you can do in the time
allowed (which will be about 10 minutes) the better.
Practise seeing how many of these three-part
sentences you can do in 10 minutes. Also make
sure that you look at the question carefully to see
if you are being asked about language features,
grammar or both.

What have I learnt?

Discuss or jot down what you now know about:

- finding language features
- commenting on language features
- finding grammar features
- commenting on grammar features
- answering the question.

Putting it into practice

- You can practise these skills with any text you come across.
- Take a few minutes to identify some language features.
- Take a few minutes to identify some grammar features.
- Practise writing sentences where you name the feature,
  give an example and make a comment.

My learning ▶

This lesson will help you to:
- identify and comment on the effects of presentational features
- identify and name structural features.

Introducing presentation and structure

Presentation

When you read something that has been published, someone has written the text and someone has decided how it's going to look – the presentation.

There are many different presentational features that you can use including:

▶ style

▶ size

▶ font

▶ graphics (pictures, graphs, logos, etc.).

The presentational features have been annotated on the text below.

GradeStudio

Examiner tip

In the exam you might be asked to:
- identify presentational and structural features and comment on their effects.

Use of logo

Main heading in bold – stands out

METRO

⊖ **Transport for London**

METRO**TRAVEL**

DLR to benefit from massive 2012 Games investment

First paragraph uses larger font and stands out with separation lines

The Docklands Light Railway (DLR) will benefit from £80million in improvements to prepare the network for the 2012 Olympic and Paralympic Games.

The enhancements will help boost annual passenger numbers from 67million to 100million by 2012. The improvements are funded by the Olympic Delivery Authority (ODA) and are outlined in its new publication, 'pace'.

The investment will contribute to schemes that expand the network, increase the number of rail cars and provide an even more reliable and frequent service. Passengers will benefit as early as 2010, when the first projects will be completed.

Four new stations – Star Lane, Abbey Road, Stratford High Street and Stratford International – will be built along the Stratford international extension, which will open in July 2010. These will give people who live in the area a better and more frequent connection to the Olympic Park and other London 2012 venues served by the DLR. They will also support the community, which has suffered from poor access to transport.

Director of the DLR, Jonathan Fox, said: 'DLR is already ahead of the game in its plans for 2012 thanks to funding and support from the ODA. The extensions and upgrades we will have in place will not only make for a successful Olympic and Paralympic Games but provide reliable and well-connected public transport for years to come.'

■ The ODA document can be downloaded from www.london2012.com/publications

Did you know?
- Around 500,000 people are expected to use the DLR on each day during the first week of the 2012 Games
- On average, 18,600 people use the DLR to Stratford Regional station every day but this will increase to 75,000 during the games
- There will be 27 DLR trains per hour on the Stratford International extension into the heart of the Olympic Park, in games time, and there will be a 25 per cent increase in the length of the DLR by 2010
- All DLR stations are step-free, there is level access between the floor of the train and platforms, and carriages are spacious, benefiting wheelchair users and passengers with mobility aids

Large colourful image to show the topic of the article and engage reader

Use of bullets breaks the text up

The article below is taken from *The Sun* newspaper. Look at it carefully and list as many presentational features as you can find. Because this is about how the text looks you don't need to read the words for meaning.

Sun

YOU CAN SELL THIS THING IF IT AIN'T GOT THAT BLING

Initials…on the gate

Pile…England star's mansion

OTT…Neville and his flash dining room

Neville must axe 'gaudy' fittings to flog home

By BEN ASHFORD

England soccer ace Phil Neville has been told to tone down his 'gaudy' mansion if he wants to sell it.

The Everton captain and wife Julie kitted out their dining room and bedroom in favourite WAG label Versace.

The proud pair also plastered their initials P and J on the front gates and carpets.

But Neville, 31, has had to slash £600,000 off the £4million price of the sprawling six-bedroom home in Crawshawbooth, Lancs, after failing to find a buyer in seven months.

Phil Spencer, presenter of Channel 4 property show *Location, Location, Location*, said: 'Anyone buying a home that gaudy and personalised would almost be obliged to change it.

'After paying that amount of money they will want to do their own thing. And it's a difficult time to sell.'

Check your answer to Activity 1. Did you identify the following? Add any that you missed to your list.

- Newspaper logo
- Headline
- Black print
- White print
- Upper case letters
- Picture
- Inset pictures
- Captions
- Underlining
- Bold font
- Italic font

In the exam you might be asked to comment on the effect of some of these presentational features. Activity 2 introduces this next stage.

GradeStudio

Examiner tips

When you are asked to comment on the effect of presentational features, the best method of answering the question is to take each feature in turn and:
- name the feature
- give an example of it from the text
- comment on its effect.

GradeStudio

Check your answer

Did you:
- number each of your points
- find four different presentational features
- make a comment about the effect of each of them?

Activity 2

Look again at the article on page 47. Take four of the presentational features that you found and make a comment about their effect. Number your features: 1, 2, 3, 4. For example, you might say:

1 The picture of Phil Neville lets the reader know what he looks like.

2 The picture of the room supports the view that the fittings are 'gaudy'.

Structure

In the activities on page 47 and above, you worked on a text where there were many different presentational devices. Sometimes there are not so many but they have been chosen in order to have a particular impact on the reader. To get started, you still need the same skills of very close observation in order to identify as many features as you can.

You might also be asked about structural features, such as the following:

- paragraphs, stanzas, bullet points, sections
- introduction, conclusion, summary, repetition
- words that help structure a text, such as *first*, *secondly*, *in conclusion*.

Activity 3

Read the newspaper article opposite and then answer the questions about the structural features that surround it. Some of the features have been labelled for you.

Headline runs across whole article to connect the different features together

Colours the same

a Why is the subheading in bold?
b What is the effect of it as a question?

What is the purpose of the headline?

Transport for London

METRO

METRO TRAVEL

DLR to benefit from massive 2012 Games investment

The Docklands Light Railway (DLR) will benefit from £80million in improvements to prepare the network for the 2012 Olympic and Paralympic Games.

(A) The enhancements will help boost annual passenger numbers from 67million to 100million by 2012. The improvements are funded by the Olympic Delivery Authority (ODA) and are outlined in its new publication, 'pace'.

(B) The investment will contribute to schemes that expand the network, increase the number of rail cars and provide an even more reliable and frequent service. Passengers will benefit as early as 2010, when the first projects will be completed.

(C) Four new stations – Star Lane, Abbey Road, Stratford High Street and Stratford International – will be built along the Stratford international extension, which will open in July 2010. These will give people who live in the area a better and more frequent connection to the Olympic Park and other London 2012 venues served by the DLR. They will also support the community, which has suffered from poor access to transport.

(D) Director of the DLR, Jonathan Fox, said: 'DLR is already ahead of the game in its plans for 2012 thanks to funding and support from the ODA. The extensions and upgrades we will have in place will not only make for a successful Olympic and Paralympic Games but provide reliable and well-connected public transport for years to come.'

■ *The ODA document can be downloaded from www.london2012.com/publications*

Did you know?

* Around 500,000 people are expected to use the DLR on each day during the first week of the 2012 Games
* On average, 18,600 people use the DLR to Stratford Regional station every day but this will increase to 75,000 during the games
* There will be 27 DLR trains per hour on the Stratford International extension into the heart of the Olympic Park, in games time, and there will be a 25 per cent increase in the length of the DLR by 2010
* All DLR stations are step-free, there is level access between the floor of the train and platforms, and carriages are spacious, benefiting wheelchair users and passengers with mobility aids

What is the purpose of the bullets?

We read from left to right. Why do you think this article has the colour image on the left, the main article in the middle and the 'Did you know?' facts on the right?

The main part of the article is split into four paragraphs. Match paragraphs A, B, C and D to the four labels below:
• Expert opinion
• Introduction
• Development
• Specific details

My learning ▶

This lesson will help you to:
- identify presentational and structural features
- comment on how these interest the reader.

Commenting on presentation and structure

In Activity 1 below there are several different presentational and structural devices at work, all of which are designed to interest the reader.

Read the text below, listing as many presentational and structural devices as you can and then answer the following question:

How do the designers of this text use presentational and structural devices to interest the reader?

Golf, basketball, ten-pin bowling… parakeet AJ has mastered them all

The above-par birdie

By **Ross McGuinnes**

Top of the tree: AJ the sporty parakeet holds a mini golf club in his beak to putt a hole-in-one to shouts of 'good job' from his trainer

IF THERE was an Olympic Games for birds, this sporty parakeet would be favourite for golds galore.

AJ is such a good all-rounder he can putt a golf ball, slam dunk a basketball and perform gymnastic routines.

Thousands of fans have watched a video of the sporty bird demonstrating his skills on the internet.

In the 1min 14sec clip, the green and yellow parrot's personal trainer shouts words of support from the sidelines with comments such as 'good bird' and 'good job'.

AJ also psyches himself up by repeating: 'Put the ball in the basket. Put the ball in the basket.'

METRO

'He is the most sporty bird in the world'

The 18-year-old Indian ringneck parakeet starts his routine by playing dead and jumping to his feet as his trainer says: 'Get up.'

He then uses a high bar to perform more remarkable flips before flying to his £2,000 miniature golf course.

The sporty bird then swings a club in his beak and the ball slides into the hole – possibly for a birdie.

Owner Dave Cota, from Florida, believes his parakeet is probably the most sporty bird in the world.

'It seems he can play anything I show him,' said the 40-year-old.

Wildlife expert Chris Packham explained the parrot species had a natural ability to learn human behaviour.

He said: 'The parrot's beak and claws, designed to grasp and open fruit, gives it a dexterity not found in all birds. Bring that together with its ability to learn and mimic and you can see why these birds are so popular.'

Flying high: The bird has also learnt how to play basket ball, roll over sideways and play tenpin bowling

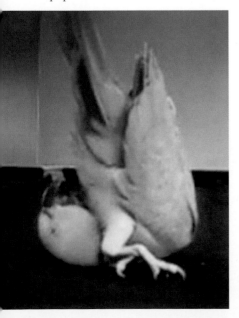

My learning ▶

This lesson will help you to:
- practise an exam-style question
- assess your answer by looking at other responses.

Assessment practice

Now you are going to have a go at an exam-style question.
Attempt the activity in the time suggested and then
complete the Peer/Self-assessment activity that follows.

First of all identify and jot down all the
presentational and structural features that you can find in
the advert below and then answer this question in 15 minutes:

**How are presentational and structural features used in
this advertisement, and what are their effects?**

Shopping

Six of the best

Headbands, chosen by Claire Foster, accessories editor to WGSN

£45

▶ A kitsch, oversized camellia
bloom is perfect for the onslaught
of summer weddings.
*Black thorn, from Anna Lou of
London, www.annalouoflondon.com,
020-7287 6975*

£65

▶ More a work of art than an
accessory. Just right for an outfit
that needs something extra.
*Luxury hairband, by Jennifer
Ouellette, available at Liberty,
www.liberty.co.uk, 020-7573 9645*

£14

▶ A 'summer of love'-style
headband adds vintage charm to
dressed-up day and
evening looks.
*Feather lace hairband, Urban Out-
fitters, www.urbanoutfitters.co.uk*

£4

▶ If you want to channel the 80s,
this woven Aztec pattern is a steal.
*Byzantine woven alice band, from
Accessorize, www.accessorize.co.uk*

The Guardian

Peer/Self-assessment activity

1 Check your answer to Activity 1. Did you:
- find several presentational features
- find several structural features
- comment on the effect of each of them?

2 Now grade your answer to Activity 1 using the mark scheme below. Before you do this you might like to read some sample answers on this activity on pages 54 and 55.

D
- identifies two or more features
- comments on both presentational and structural features
- some extra material.

C
- clear and effective attempt to engage with activity
- range of relevant points
- both presentational and structural features covered
- comments on both presentational and structural features.

B
- clear and effective engagement with activity
- range of relevant points
- clear understanding of effects of features.

£23

▶ This dove band is a sweet nod to the trend for hair jewellery.
Clear dove headband, from Buddug, www.buddug.com

£100

▶ Mixing prim **schoolgirl chic with** quirky decoration, this is a new way to **wear** nuts and bolts.
Black with pearl and screws, from Marc by Marc Jacobs, www. marcjacobs.com, 020-7399 1690

GradeStudio

Here are two student answers to the activity on page 52.
How are presentational and structural features used in this advertisement, and what are their effects?
Read the answers together with the examiner comments. Then check what you have learnt and try putting it into practice.

Student A

True, but not relevant to task

Something about effect but not related either to structure or to presentation

True, but not about either structure or presentation

Presentational feature but vague and general

> This advertisement is about headbands. It is rather boring because it isn't about anything that interests me. It gives some information about costs and there are pictures of five headbands. There is a bit of colour to it but <u>not very much.</u> The headline is in pink showing it is aimed at girls. The advertisement doesn't appeal to me and I wouldn't buy any of these headbands.

Not accurate

General comment on effect but not related to either structure or presentation

Identifies presentational feature

Examiner comment

This answer identifies two presentational features but nothing on structure. There are some general comments on the effect on the reader but they are not related closely either to presentation or structure. Less than half of what is written is relevant to the task. The second to last sentence just lifts the answer into the D band because of the identification of a second presentational device and an appropriate comment on it.

 grade answer

Student B

Structure and effect

Presentation and detail

Effect

Point developed

Presentation and purpose

> The advertisement is meant to look interesting because it isn't symmetrically arranged. The prices are in a large, different coloured font, which makes them stand out and grab the reader's attention. The names and where to get them from are in italics underneath, meant to separate this information off. The colours are dull. Maybe they are meant to look 'cool' but they don't appeal to me.

Structure

Effect

Presentation

Examiner comment

This answer has a range of clear points about presentation and structure, each supported by a detail and each with a comment about effect. It is well into the C band.

 MOVING UP THE GRADES

Presentational and structural features

To move up the grades, make sure you identify features in the activity before you read the text. Then for each feature that you mention, name the feature, give an example and make a comment. This will keep you on track throughout your answer and the more of these you can do in the time allowed (which will be about 10 minutes) the better. Practise seeing how many of these three-part sentences you can do in 10 minutes. Also make sure that you look at the question carefully to see if you are being asked about presentational features, structure or both.

What have I learnt?

Discuss or jot down what you now know about:
- finding presentational features
- commenting on presentational features
- finding structural features
- commenting on structural features
- answering the question.

Putting it into practice

- You can practise these skills with any text you come across.
- Take a few minutes to identify some presentational features.
- Take a few minutes to identify some structural features.
- Practise writing sentences where you name the feature, give an example and make a comment.

My learning ▶

This lesson will help you to:
- make comparisons within and between texts
- select material to answer the question.

Introducing collating and comparing

Collate

Collate means putting more than one thing together. If the exam question is aimed at the 'collate' part of this Assessment Objective, you might be asked to choose your own material from several texts and then answer an activity based on the material you have chosen.

Compare

One of the questions in the Reading paper is very likely to ask you to **compare**. This means:

▶ find similarities

▶ find differences

▶ find similarities within differences

▶ find differences within similarities.

You don't know before you see the question paper what you are going to be asked to compare. It might be, for example:

▶ how information is presented in more than one text

▶ the purpose of and audience for more than one text

▶ how language is used

▶ presentational devices

▶ the similarities and differences between two similar stories.

Note: if the question asks you to make 'cross-references' – this means make comparisons.

GradeStudio

Examiner tips

In the exam you are likely to be asked to:
- compare material in two texts
- make a comparison by choosing which texts to compare.

GradeStudio

Examiner tips

- Always find your material in the two texts first. Then find some clear similarities and some clear differences.
- These words and phrases are sometimes useful when you are comparing:
  both texts...   each text...
  on the other hand...   however....

Practising collating

This first activity does **not** ask you to compare. You need to find three headlines that you can say more than one thing about and then do each one in turn.

Activity 1

Read the newspaper headlines below and then answer the following question:

How do the writers and designers of three of these headlines try to make the reader want to read the article?

You are given five headlines, but only asked to write about three. So you need to:

- look closely at all five
- think which three you could say the most about
- try to find at least two things to say about those you have chosen.

PHIL THE CRACKS!
Players turning on Scolari

I CANUTE BELIEVE IT, MY HOME IS SAVED

Bring back the beaver – he will save money and clean our rivers

Vince swims against the sea of sewage

Home Tweet Home

GradeStudio

Check your answer

Did you:
- choose three headlines
- write about each one in turn
- consider language
- consider print sizes, fonts, upper and lower case?

Practising comparing

Activity 2 uses the same headlines as Activity 1 but **does** ask you to compare. You might decide that as you have to compare you would choose different headlines in order to find some similarities and differences.

Here's some advice to help you complete Activity 2.

▶ You only have to compare two headlines at a time. So, if we call them 1, 2 and 3 the best way is to compare 1 with 2, then compare 1 with 3 and finally compare 2 with 3.

▶ There may be some things all three headlines have in common, though, so you could also put that.

▶ There may be some things which are different in all three so you could put that too.

Activity 2

Remind yourself of the headlines and advice above and then answer the following question:

Compare the ways in which the writers and designers of three of these headlines try to make the reader want to read the article.

GradeStudio

Check your answer

Did you:
- make a comparison in each sentence
- find several similarities
- find several differences
- make your points clear to the reader?

My learning ▶

This lesson will help you to:
- compare texts
- select material to answer the question.

Developing comparisons

The activities in this lesson require you to first make comparisons between two texts and then within one text.

This task asks you to compare two accounts of the same story. The stories are about the same event and appeared in different newspapers on the same day.
Read the texts below and opposite and then complete the following task.

Compare the ways this story is presented. Write about:
- **the information**
- **the headlines**
- **the language**
- **the presentational devices.**

GradeStudio

Examiner tips

To succeed with Activity 1:
- compare the texts all the way through your answer
- deal with each of the four bullets
- cover similarities and differences.

It's a plant, officer
DRUG RAID OVER SMELLY FLOWERS

High jinx ... top, where plant grew, front door and, right, Ivor in garage

By JOHN COLES

DRUG squad cops raided an elderly couple because a plant in their garden smelled like CANNABIS.

Shocked Ivor and Margaret Wiltshire returned from holiday to find their front door kicked in and their house and garage searched.

The police left empty-handed because the tell-tale smell was caused by a tiny creeping flower called Moss Phlox.

It was the **SECOND** time the pongy plant had been mistaken for pot.

Four days before the police raid, the Wiltshire's neighbours David and Christine Difford were terrified when a gang wearing Hallowe'en masks turned up demanding drugs.

David, 54, said: 'They shouted, "Give us the weed, man" and searched the loft. It was frightening.'

Retired engineer Ivor, 77, dug up the Phlox and has received an apology from police, who said the raid followed 'other investigations'.

Ivor, who has no sense of smell, said in Kingswood, Bristol: 'We can't believe such a small plant has caused so much trouble.'

POT THE DIFFERENCE

DOPE

PHLOX

Dopes!

OAPS RAIDED FOR GROWING PLANT THAT SMELLS LIKE POT

WRONG MOSS PHLOX

RIGHT CANNABIS

BY GEOFFREY LAKEMAN

POLICE smashed down the front door of an OAP couple to swoop on their 'cannabis' horde – a sweet-smelling £2 plant bought from the garden centre.

Ivor and Margaret Wiltshire, 77 and 79, bought the moss phlox four years ago but it was only this summer that the pink plant gave off a pungent aroma similar to cannabis.

And the smell was so strong their next-door neighbours were even threatened by a drug gang who broke in and demanded: 'Give us the weed.' And weeks later Ivor and Margaret came home from holiday in October to find the door battered down and the drug squad inside. The grandfather-of-three, who has had no sense of smell since an operation 30 years ago, said: 'It multiplied fast. I was happy because it looked so nice.

I haven't got any idea what cannabis smells like and certainly never smoked it.

'I was so distressed that I felt like digging up the whole garden. We can't believe such a small plant has caused so much trouble.'

The couple even noticed a police helicopter hovering in Kingswood, Bristol – now thought to have been using infrared to find the heat source of the cannabis 'factory'.

And neighbours David and Christine Difford, 54 and 56, said of the terrifying raid by a masked gang: 'They were very keen to look in the loft which left me baffled. But I'm not surprised at the police raid. You could smell it all the way up the road.' Avon and Somerset police, which is investigating, said: 'We received a complaint and have apologised.'

> I've no idea what cannabis smells like. I've certainly never smoked it
> IVOR WILTSHIRE

Daily Mirror

Comparing within a text

Activity 1 was a broad activity that meant you had to be careful to select material to cover all the bullets and to make comparisons. You might get a very tight activity, though, with much less material to choose from. You might also get an activity where you are asked to compare within a text. Activity 2 is an example of this type of activity.

Activity 2

Read the text below and then answer the following question:

Compare the language used in the first seven paragraphs with the language used by Sarah Colclough and Nigel Pickard within the article.

What are the effects on the reader of these differences?

DAILY STAR

KIDS TV GETS TOUCHY-FEELY

Tots tune in to Hippy-Tubbies

■ by VICTORIA RICHARDS

TV's new Tellytubby-style characters are a bunch of tree-hugging hippies.

The touchy-feely series *Waybuloo* sees fluffy family the Piplings doing yoga and embracing each other.

The show for toddlers stars four animated characters, Lau Lau, De Li, Nok Tok and Yojojo.

Each character, representing a particular quality or emotion, bounces through a cartoon countryside trying to achieve a state of happiness called Buloo.

Simple

If they feel truly happy or make their pals feel better they begin to float.

They even interact with children – known as Cheebies – by addressing toddlers and parents at home.

Those watching are encouraged to join in with 'yogo' exercises, which are simple yoga moves for two to five-year-olds.

Sarah Colclough, executive producer for CBeebies, said 'We were looking for a concept that would bring together that elusive notion of children's emotions.

'It is an extremely distinctive programme in that way. Each show teaches about friendship, co-operation and citizenship,' she added.

OLD SCHOOL: Tellytubbies

'The heart of the programme is about encouraging children to be happy. At the launch the children watching were utterly mesmerised.'

Nigel Pickard, director of family entertainment at programme maker RDF, said Waybuloo would show children how they can 'work together to become positive and content'.

This lesson will help you to:
- practise an exam-style question
- assess your answer by looking at other responses.

Assessment practice

Now you are going to have a go at an exam-style question. Attempt the activity in the time suggested and then complete the Peer/Self-assessment activity that follows.

Activity 1

Read the following two texts, which both feature the Queen, then spend 15 minutes answering this question:

Compare these two texts in terms of their:
- **purpose and audience**
- **language**
- **presentation**.

DAILY STAR

UNION JACKASSES
8ft pole too dangerous to fly flag for hero Brit troops

■ by JERRY LAWTON

BUREAU-PRATS have banned the Union flag from flying in honour of our troops because the 8ft pole is too dangerous to climb.

For 453 years a flag has proudly flown over the Town Hall in Bourne, Lincs, to mark Armed Forces Day and the Queen's birthday.

But now the council has banned it on health and safety grounds.

Town hall bigwigs say it is too risky for a member of staff to climb a ladder to unfurl the flag.

They have also banned the flag of St George on patron saint's day.

Fury erupted last night as residents and war veterans condemned the move.

Former mayor Brian Fines, 72, a former Army Lieutenant Colonel, raged: 'What a sad and sick society we're becoming.

Life

'This despotic government's health and safety laws have prevented the council flying a flag from the building that's the hub of our town.

'We are told they're not allowed to use a ladder to access the mast. It's annoying and upsetting a lot of people.'

Councillor Fines spent 30 years with the Royal Electrical and Mechanical Engineers before running engineering firms in the private sector.

He said: 'I've been in charge of engineering businessesemploying hundreds of people. Health and safety has been my bread and butter.

'But it shouldn't be about someone sitting in an office and saying no.

'It seems it's permeating every aspect of life. It's like a cancer.'

Mayor Shirley Cliffe said: 'I just don't understand it. A lot of the public are upset.

'It's the first time the flag won't be flown. It's disgusting. It's essential that we fly the flag to help celebrate occasions such as these.'

It's 'too risky' to fly flag in Bourne

Local decorator Phil Sargent, 47, added: 'If climbing ladders is so dangerous I'd have been out of business or dead years ago.'

A spokesman for South Kesteven District Council insisted: 'The process involves our site manager climbing an 8ft ladder which rests on a plinth overlooking a spiked gate. We think this is too risky.'

Sport of Queens

There is democratic glory and no shame in being a royal also-ran at the Festival

Come on Barbers Shop. You were in there with a chance, but you dropped back over the last three fences. The Queen's colours were fluttered in the Cheltenham Gold Cup for the first time yesterday. And even the ranks of Ireland could scarce forbear to cheer. When they inherited George VI's stable, the Queen took the Flat, and her mother the Jumps. The Queen, an infrequent visitor, was last at Cheltenham six years ago to unveil the bust of her mother. She had ring-fenced her engagements yesterday in order to watch Barbers Shop, whom she inherited from her mother, jump well; but just not well enough.

Horses and royals go together like divorce and marriage. For racing is the one sport where the monarchy plays on a fairly level track beside its subjects. Both horses and royalty depend on bloodlines. Both royalty and horses rely on the affection of the punters and the support of bookies, or ministers. Both are constrained to run down constitutional rails between prescribed limits with regular turns, jumps or hurdles.

Boadicea was the first equestrian queen to be recorded in the form book, though the Roman Jockey Club considered the scythes on her chariot wheels an early example of nobbling. Henry VIII imported the royal stud; Charles II wrote the rules for racing at Newmarket; Queen Anne invented royal Ascot, and rode down the course in her best hat to start the meeting. Democracy has replaced absolute monarchy. But hippocracy – horses rule, OK? – is still a British peculiar.

Yesterday the Queen experienced Cheltenham: to race, to jump, to bet and not to win. But has she caught the spring fever of a national celebration? Better luck next year, Ma'am.

THE TIMES

Peer/Self-assessment activity

1 Check your answer to Activity 1. Did you:
- compare their purposes
- compare their audiences
- compare their content
- find several language features to comment on
- find several presentation features to comment on?

2 Now grade your answer to Activity 1 using the mark scheme below. Before you do this you might like to read some sample answers on this activity on pages 64 and 65.

D
- ▶ identifies two or more features
- ▶ some attempt to compare
- ▶ some extra material.

C
- ▶ clear attempt to engage with activity
- ▶ range of relevant comparisons
- ▶ all three bullets covered.

B
- ▶ clear and effective engagement with activity
- ▶ range of structured comparisons
- ▶ clear understanding of all three bullets.

Here are two student answers to the activity on page 62.
Compare these two texts in terms of their:
• *purpose and audience*   • *language*   • *presentation*.
Read the answers together with the examiner comments. Then check what you have
learnt and try putting it into practice.

D grade answer

Student A

Comparison

Comparison of
presentation feature

The only thing these texts have in common is that they mention the
Queen. There is a picture of her in the *Daily Star* article, but not in *The
Times*. The article in *The Times* is all writing but the *Daily Star* has pictures
to make it more interesting. Both articles seem to like the Queen.

Comparison of
presentation feature

Attempts effect but
doesn't compare
purpose or audience

General
comparison

Examiner comment

There is some comparison here and a little detail. Only some of the
bullets are covered, though, and most points are very general. It is
really only the start to a decent answer. It falls just into the D band.

Comparison

Supported with details

Presentation feature

Supported

Turned into a comparison

Comparison of audience

Supported

The text from *The Times* is an article about the Queen and horse racing. The other one also mentions the Queen because it is about flying a flag to celebrate the Queen's birthday and it has a picture of the Queen, but the article is about a flag pole being too dangerous to fly the flag. There are two pictures in the article from the *Daily Star* but none in *The Times*, so the *Daily Star* article is more for people who want to be entertained. The *Daily Star* article is for people who don't like to read as much as the people reading *The Times*. *The Times* has some language devices in it, like the rule of three with three sentences beginning with 'Both' and a sentence breaking the rules by beginning with 'And' but the *Daily Star* has some puns instead like 'Union Jackasses' and 'Bureau-prats'. Both articles have headlines but the one in *The Times* is much more formal because it doesn't have jokes in it.

Comparison of presentation feature

Supported

Language and grammar features

Examiner comment

This is a clear attempt to engage with the task. It makes several comparisons and covers all the bullets. It supports most of its points by reference to the text's details. It is in the C band.

Collate and compare

To move up the grades, make sure you identify the key words in the activity before you read the text. Then for each comparison that you make:

· name the feature
· give an example
· make a comment.

This will keep you on track throughout your answer and the more of these you can do in the time allowed (which will be about 10 minutes) the better. Practise seeing how many of these three-part sentences you can do in 10 minutes.

What have I learnt?

Discuss or jot down what you now know about:
· collating and choosing texts
· comparing texts
· answering the question.

Putting it into practice

· You can practise these skills with any text you come across.
· Take a few minutes to compare the content of two texts.
· Compare the purposes of and audiences for two texts.
· Compare the language used.
· Compare the presentation features used.

Section B
Writing

Introduction

This section aims to encourage you to develop your writing skills. The teaching, texts, activities and tips are all focused on helping you achieve the best grade you can in your exam.

This part of your course encourages you to write for different purposes and audiences and to make some choices about how you write. Successful writers make all kinds of choices: not just who they are writing for and the purpose of the text, but what kind of language would be best to use and what kinds of presentational devices would help the reader to take in what is written.

We write all the time, but what we write isn't always formal. We write lists, notes for people, text messages and emails to friends. But these also have their own conventions and they are no use if they can't be understood by the person reading them.

So writing clearly and appropriately is what we all need to achieve as much of the time as possible.

The different chapters in this section look at specific aspects of writing, one at a time. But we don't often write like this. We need to have in mind all the different skills all the time and that is what this book is aiming to help you do.

In the exam you will have to do two pieces of writing, most probably for different purposes and maybe for different audiences, so practising the skills individually in the following chapters will help you to have all the different skills in place when the day of the exam comes.

Assessment Objectives

The Assessment Objectives underpin everything you will learn about and be tested upon. It is vital that you understand what these are asking of you. So, here are the Assessment Objectives that relate to the Writing part of your exam together with comments to help you understand what they are.

► Write to communicate clearly and effectively using and adapting forms and selecting vocabulary appropriate to task and purpose in ways that engage the reader.

► Organise information and ideas into structured and sequenced sentences, paragraphs and whole texts, using a variety of linguistic and structural features to support cohesion and overall coherence.

► Use a range of sentence structures for clarity, purpose and effect, with accurate punctuation and spelling.

This Assessment Objective asks you to make what you have to say clear and to write in such a way that the readers will be interested in what you write because you have chosen appropriate and interesting language.

This Assessment Objective means that the whole text needs to hang together. Paragraphs, particularly links between paragraphs, will help you to do this as will writing which is clearly organised and sequenced. You are writing in timed conditions in the exam, but you always need to think about how long your text needs to be to do the job properly, so that it ends up just the right length for the readers to take in what you need them to take in.

This final Assessment Objective is about technical accuracy and variety. This is where many students fail to do as well as they could because they don't proof read their writing carefully enough. Remember that in the exam it's the quality and accuracy of the writing that matter. Crossings out are fine if you find during your checking that you can make improvements and corrections.

Examiner and student concerns

To help you improve your grades it is helpful to know what concerns examiners and students most about the Writing section of the exam. Below is a list of some of the concerns that they have.

What concerns examiners?

▶ Clear focus on the task throughout. Some answers have too much material which is not necessary; others don't develop their points.

▶ Technical errors such as spelling and punctuation.

▶ It's not always easy to see where the writing is going.

▶ Students sometimes write all they can think of rather than selecting what is going to be most effective.

What concerns students?

▶ How much should I write?

▶ I don't have time to check.

▶ Teachers always tell us to plan but there's not enough time.

▶ I have so much to say I just want to get it all down.

Writing in the exam

There are several things you need to consider when you are doing a writing activity in the exam. You need to think about:

▶ what exactly the question is asking you to do

▶ the purpose of the text you are writing

▶ the audience it is for

▶ how to structure your answer

▶ how to use appropriate language

▶ what presentational devices you need to use

▶ how to interest the reader in what you write.

Activity 1

Opposite are the opening paragraphs from two student answers to the following activity:

Argue for or against school uniform.

Read the student answers opposite, together with the activity that they are responding to. Think about which answer interests you more and why. Then complete the questions below.

1 Which of these makes you interested in reading on?

2 What techniques does it use to do so?

3 In what ways is the other one not really answering the question, even in the first paragraph?

4 Which uses language more effectively? What techniques has it used?

5 Which uses a variety of sentence structures more effectively? What kinds of sentences has it used?

6 Which shows some individuality and personality?

7 Which shows more clarity and imagination?

8 Which is more accurate technically?

Student A

Clear statements arguing for school uniform, beginning to explain

Some people think that it is a good idea for pupils to wear school uniform. This is because they all then look the same and members of the public can tell what school they come from. This might be useful if they are in any trouble. On the other hand, other people think that school uniform is unnecessary because it makes everyone look the same and they are not the same. They are individuals.

Explains some arguments against but not asked for in task

Now against – not the task which was for or against

Student B

Rhetorical question introduces argument against school uniform

Unusual opening with clear image

Wide and interesting, varied vocabulary

Green striped blazers and green and white ties. What could be more hideous? Instead of promoting social equality it brands all teenagers as stereotyped and ugly. How can schools expect their pupils to form good judgements, develop taste and individuality when the poor children are all forced to wear the same clothes which they would never in their wildest dreams choose to wear?

Wide and interesting, varied vocabulary

Longer rhetorical question, complex argument; argument against school uniform clearly established

What did the examiner think?

Student B answers the question whereas Student A starts by arguing both for **and** against rather than for **or** against.

Student B's work is significantly better, more varied and more interesting than Student A's. But they are both accurate technically. There aren't any spelling or punctuation mistakes in either, although Student A doesn't use sentence forms for effect and only uses full stops and one comma. The examiner is unlikely to have read many like Student B's work before and so is interested in what it is going to say. He or she will probably have read dozens and dozens like Student A's.

Student A's is a D response whereas Student B's is a B.

My learning ▶

This lesson will help you to:
- plan, write and check effectively in different forms and for different audiences
- adapt the level of formality in your writing.

Writing clearly, effectively and imaginatively

The way you write will depend very much on the audience and purpose of your text. This means that you might well choose different kinds of language and sentence structures if the audience is different.

Activity 1

Here is some information, in a random order, about Hampton Court. Read the information and then complete the task that follows.

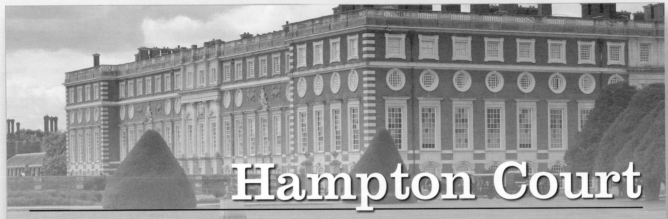

Hampton Court

- It was extended in the late 17th century for William and Mary. The new buildings were designed by Sir Christopher Wren.
- Henry VIII rebuilt and enlarged the palace after 1530.
- Hampton Court is by the Thames in Hampton in south west London.
- Queen Victoria opened the palace to the public in 1838.
- It was built by Cardinal Wolsey and begun in 1514.
- The original chimney pots are all different from each other.

- The nursery rhyme 'Mary, Mary, quite contrary' refers to the rebuilding of Hampton Court for Queen Mary.
- The original Tudor kitchens are well worth a visit.
- Queen Mary was a keen gardener and had the gardens at Hampton Court redesigned.
- The maze dates from 1714.
- The palace is huge and even though you can only visit a small part of it, a thorough visit takes a whole day.

GradeStudio

Check your answer

Did you:
- think carefully about the audience and purpose of your text
- number the points before you began in order to sequence them properly
- present the information clearly
- use some persuasive language?

Write a short entry about Hampton Court for a tourist guide. Make sure that you:
- give the information in a clear and logical order
- interest the reader by using your own words when you want to
- persuade the reader that Hampton Court would be a good place to visit.

In Activity 2, you need to write about Hampton Court again, but this time in a different form – an email to a relative.

Activity 2

Now use the same information, from Activity 1, to write for a very different audience (a specific one this time) and a different purpose:

Imagine that a relative has told you that they are going to be visiting London for a few days and that they have asked you to recommend somewhere interesting to visit. Write an email to your relative explaining why you think they should visit Hampton Court.

Because this is an email to a relative you might well want to use some less formal language. How informal your language is will, of course, depend on what your relative is like and how they would expect you to write.

For example, to a relative you know well you might write:

You've got to see Hampton Court – it's fab!

Whereas, a more formal example might be:

You really should visit Hampton Court as it is one of London's best attractions.

GradeStudio

Examiner tip

- You don't have to include all the information about Hampton Court this time. Select what you think is appropriate but make sure that you explain why your relative should visit.

GradeStudio

Check your answer

Did you:

- select material appropriate for your relative
- explain why he or she should visit
- use a range of sentence structures
- use interesting vocabulary
- check your work for accuracy in punctuation, spelling and grammar?

This lesson will help you to:
- assess, mark and grade an answer
- apply the learning to your own work.

Assessment practice

Peer/Self-assessment activity

Read the response, opposite, by a student in timed conditions to the following activity:

Write an article for a teenage magazine in which you persuade the readers not to smoke.

1 Looking at the student's response, answer the following questions.

Communication and organisation
a Is it aimed at teenagers?
b Does it persuade them not to smoke?
c Are the different points sequenced as well as they could be?
d Is language used effectively to persuade?
e Is there a wide range of interesting vocabulary?

Sentence structure, punctuation and spelling
f Has a variety of sentence structures been used?
g Are there some sentence forms for effect?
h Are the paragraphs in reasonable places?
i Are there any links between paragraphs?
j How accurate is the spelling? Find the errors.
k How accurate is the punctuation? Find the errors.
l How many different kinds of punctuation marks are used?

2 Now you've looked carefully at this student response and thought about the different elements in it, you are in a position to try to apply the mark scheme.

Take each mark scheme descriptor in turn and work out which you think most closely matches what you have read. This is what the examiners do. Then decide on a grade and explain why you think it is that grade.

3 Once you have marked and graded the student's answer, complete the 'What have I learnt?' activity on page 73.

Communication and organisation

D
- conscious attempt to suit needs of purpose and audience
- begins to engage reader's response
- clear if mechanical paragraphs
- some selection of vocabulary for effect.

C
- clear identification with purpose and audience
- begins to sustain reader's response
- clear selection of vocabulary for effect
- clear accurate paragraphs.

B
- form, content and style are generally matched to purpose and audience
- increasing sophistication in vocabulary choice and phrasing
- effective paragraphing with links between paragraphs.

Sentence structure, punctuation and spelling

D
- uses a range of securely marked out sentence structures
- some accurate spelling of more complex words
- uses a range of punctuation.

C
- uses some sentence forms for effect
- generally secure in spelling
- generally secure in punctuation.

B
- uses sentence forms for effect
- accurate spelling
- accurate punctuation.

Student A

The act of smoking,

In many case smoking has lead to heart problems, lung throat and mouth cancer. Although there has been a decrease of smoking, among 15 year olds from 30% to around 23%. It is still a major problem for teenagers in britain to quit smoking. The easiest way is to not to start! However if you have, there is some urges from this magazine to stop smoking. A poll from around britain shows tat 1 in 3 of all smokers started smoking from early teens. This is a health hazard and can lead to severe problems later on in life. Could you really afford to put yourself through all that pain later on in life? Just for around 10 seconds of enjoyment a day.

Many teenagers only start smoking because their friends are, they are pressured into it or use it to calm themselves down. Is this worth taking 15 minutes off your life everytime you smoke 1 ciggarette? Smoking can't be good for you, if it causes all this damage to your body why do it?

Smoking can lead to stunting your growth and your finger tips to turn yellow. Is it really necessary, to be cool you have to smell bad, stop growing and have yellow finger tips. nice. The meaning of cool has changed a lot since my day. One of the main factors of smoking is that it makes not just you but everything and every one around you smell of smoke.

I don't know if you can live with yourself smoking for fun and killing yourself, but killing everyone around you, I couldn't live with myself for doing that.

Writing clearly, effectively and imaginatively

To move up the grades, remember:
- the closer you can match your writing to purpose and audience the better
- to make sure your meaning is always clear
- to choose your language carefully to interest the reader.

What have I learnt?

Discuss or jot down what you now know about:
- what the examiners are looking for
- what a mark scheme looks like
- what you are being assessed on in your writing.

Putting it into practice

- You can work through the skills one by one in the chapters that follow.

My learning ▶

This lesson will help you to:
- plan your writing
- sequence your information and ideas.

How to organise information and ideas

Successful writing

There are four key stages towards a successful piece of writing:

1 thinking
2 planning
3 writing
4 checking.

Most students have done a lot of work on all four of these when they are preparing for the exam, but when the day comes, often they only do one of them. They write. But thinking your ideas through first and then sequencing and organising them is the real key to success. If you have your ideas ready then you can concentrate on writing them as well as you can and you can make choices about your words, sentences and paragraphs.

Sentence structures

Pages 110–113 look specifically at using four different kinds of sentence structures:

▶ simple sentences
▶ compound sentences
▶ complex sentences
▶ minor sentences.

You need to be able to use all four of these so if you are not yet confident with sentence structures look carefully at these pages.

Paragraphing

Paragraphs help the reader follow what you are saying because you are dividing your writing into sections. Effective paragraphing:

▶ divides the writing into sections to make for easy reading
▶ introduces new aspects of the topic in new paragraphs
▶ has links between the paragraphs to help the reader to follow what you are writing.

How you use paragraphs depends on what kind of text you are writing. For example:

▶ tabloid newspapers tend to use short paragraphs
▶ broadsheet newspapers tend to use longer paragraphs
▶ other articles vary the length of their paragraphs.

So first of all you need to think about what kind of text you are writing. Then you need to develop your ideas. You can do this in the form of a list or a spidergram. Activity 1 gives you the opportunity to practise these points.

Activity 1

Imagine that you have been asked to write an article for a weekend colour supplement about living a healthy lifestyle. Planning is vital because it will help you to decide where your paragraphs are going to be. This activity is all about planning – preparing you for Activity 3.

1 Decide on your audience(s) – who you are writing for. This will be mainly adults because the magazine comes with a Sunday newspaper. The article will be for a general readership.

2 Develop your ideas on the different aspects of the topic which you can cover. Do this in the form of either a list or a spidergram.

Here are some possible ideas:

- get enough sleep
- look after yourself
- eat healthily
- go to the gym
- think positively
- reduce stress.

- have treats and rewards
- keep up-to-date with work
- avoid snacking
- do aerobic exercise
- avoid eating too much

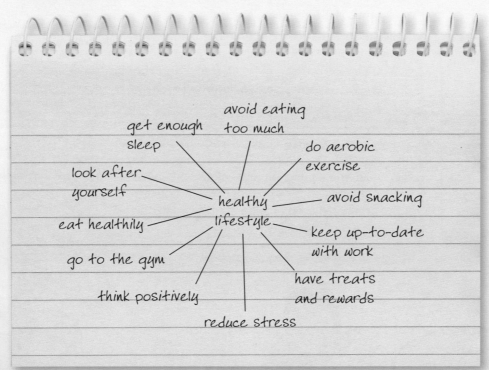

3 Decide which order to present your ideas in. Number the points in your plan. This will give you the sequence of your paragraphs. Ask yourself these questions.

- Which ideas go together?
- Which can I combine?
- Which show different aspects of the topic?

4 Decide on your headline. Make sure it's suitable for the magazine you are writing for. You might want to leave some space to put in your headline at the end.

5 Decide whether the sort of article you are writing needs subheadings. It's an issue to think about before you start to write.

Beginnings and endings

Your first and last sentences are really important. You want to grab the reader's attention with your first sentence to make the reader want to read on. For example:

Banish the lard and get fit.

is a much more interesting opening sentence than:

In this article I am going to write about being healthy by losing weight.

In the same way the last sentence needs to round off your topic and give the reader something to remember. For example:

Blueberries and tofu it is, then, rather than pizza and chips.

is much more memorable than:

Eating healthy food will do you more good than eating fatty foods.

Activity 2

Look back at the plan you made for Activity 1. Now decide on:

- your first sentence to grab the reader's interest
- your last sentence.

Make sure that you can grab the reader's interest in the first sentence and think about a catchy way to end the article. You can, of course, revise your first and your last sentence when you are checking your writing at the end.

GradeStudio

Check your answer

Did you:

- plan carefully enough
- sequence your ideas
- find links between your paragraphs
- check your answer when you had finished writing
- correct any errors of spelling, punctuation, grammar and sentence structure?

Activity 3

You should have completed all the planning in Activity 1. Now write your own article for a Sunday newspaper supplement about living a healthy lifestyle.

Lanhydrock

♿ ♿ ✝ 🚹 ⛺ 🦌 (in woods and park)

Map ref: 9

- Magnificent late Victorian country house, atmospheric home of the Agar-Robartes family
- Fifty rooms to explore, revealing fascinating aspects of life & the inner workings of this wealthy well-run household
- Highlights incl. great kitchen, evocative nursery wing & 17th century Long Gallery with plaster ceiling depicting biblical scenes
- Large formal & woodland garden incl. Victorian parterre, stunning magnolias, camellias & rhododendrons
- Superb parkland setting in the Fowey valley, with miles of walks through woods & along the river

Gift Aid Admission: Adult £9.90, child £4.95, family £24.75, family (1 adult) £14.85. Groups adult £8.40. Garden & grounds only: adult £5.60, child £2.80.

Nr Bodmin PL30 5AD
E lanhydrock@nationaltrust.org.uk
T 01208 265950 (estate 265211)
⇌ Bodmin Parkway 1¾ miles, lovely walk

The great house of Cornwall: 'Upstairs Downstairs' brought to life

Opening arrangements 2008			NB: Bold – open						
House	15 Mar–2 Nov	11–5.30 (5 from 1 Oct)	M	**T**	**W**	**T**	**F**	**S**	**S**
Garden	All year	10–6	**M**	**T**	**W**	**T**	**F**	**S**	**S**
Shop & refreshments	5 Jan–3 Feb	11–4	M	T	W	T	F	**S**	**S**
	9 Feb–14 Mar	11–4	**M**	**T**	**W**	**T**	**F**	**S**	**S**
	15 Mar–2 Nov	11–5.30 (5 from 1 Oct)	**M**	**T**	**W**	**T**	**F**	**S**	**S**
	3 Nov–24 Dec	11–4	**M**	**T**	**W**	**T**	**F**	**S**	**S**
	27 Dec–31 Dec	11–4	**M**	**T**	W	T	**F**	**S**	**S**

Also open BH Mons & Mons in August. Plant sales open daily 1 Mar – 2 Nov. Refreshments available from 10.30 in main season. Shop & refreshments are inside tariff area. Tel. for specific details of restaurant opening,

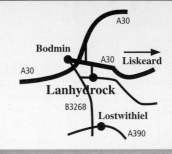

GradeStudio

Check your answer

- How clear is the information?
- How attractively is it presented?
- Have you included a range of information?
- Did you remember to use persuasive language to make the reader want to visit?

Using language and structure

It is always useful to have some models in mind when writing your own text. All of the texts in the Reading section of this book can be useful to you when you are writing your own text.

Activity 1

Read the following letter, written to a newspaper by a fireman, explaining why his work is worth the £30,000 a year he is paid. This text is full of interesting structural and language techniques. Find an example of each of the following and say what effect each has on the reader:

1 four clear sections
2 rhetorical question
3 rhetorical question repeated later
4 repeated use of 'I have'
5 triplets (groups of three)
6 repeated words within sentences
7 words repeated in related sentences
8 play on words
9 slang for dramatic effect
10 emotional appeals to the reader.

The Guardian

Am I worth £30,000?

Am I worth £30,000? In my career I have been taught skills to save life, prolong life and to know when to walk away when there is no life left. I have taken courses to fight fire from within, above and below. I can cut a car apart in minutes and I can educate your sons and daughters to save their own lives.

No matter what the emergency, I am part of a team that always comes when you call. I run in when all my instincts tell me to run away. I have faced death in cars with petrol pouring over me while the engine was ticking with the heat. I have lain on my back inside a house fire and watched the flames roar across the ceiling above me. I have climbed and I have crawled to save life and I have stood and wept while we buried a fellow firefighter.

I have been the target for yobs throwing stones and punches at me while I do my job. I have been the first person to intercept a parent who knows their son is in the car we are cutting up, and I know he is dead. I have served my time, damaged my body and seen things that I hope you never will. I have never said 'No, I'm more important than you', and walked away.

Am I worth £30k? Maybe now your answer is no. But when that drunk smashes into your car, or the candle burns down too low, or your child needs help, you will find I'm worth every last penny.

Jay Curson
Firefighter, Nottingham

Activity 2

Now imagine that you are doing a job which you think is useful and important. Write a letter to a magazine, persuading the readers that what you do is important and that it is well worth the money you earn.

- Make sure that you find your ideas first.
- Then number them in the order you can use them.
- Decide where your paragraphs are going to be.
- Make sure that you have:
  - an interesting opening
  - three or four paragraphs in the middle
  - a punchy conclusion.
- Use persuasive language features, such as those listed on page 82, to persuade the reader that your job is important.

GradeStudio

Examiner tips

- Use some of the devices that were used in the letter.
- Address the reader directly.
- Give information about your job.
- Persuade the reader that your job is worth the money you earn.

GradeStudio

Check your answer

Did you:
- structure your letter carefully
- address the reader directly
- give sufficient information
- persuade by your choices of language?

My learning objectives ▶

This lesson will help you to:
- practise your writing focusing on language and structure
- assess your answer by looking at other responses.

Assessment practice

Complete the following activity and then the Peer/Self-assessment activity that follows.

Activity 1

Now write your own text, thinking carefully about structure and language. You can choose either to:

Write the script for a speech to be given to your school or college assembly, persuading them to support the charity of your choice.

Or

Write the script for a speech to be given to your school or college assembly, persuading them to take an interest in the sport of your choice.

Grade**Studio**

Examiner tips

Before you attempt Activity 1, here are some tips that will help you to write your script.

- Gather your ideas on your chosen subject in a list or spidergram. What can you say to persuade your audience?

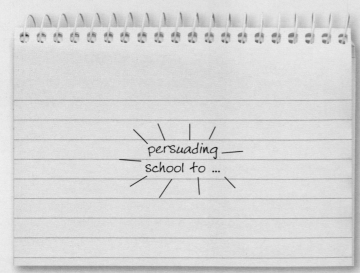

- Think of how to structure your speech. You need to include:

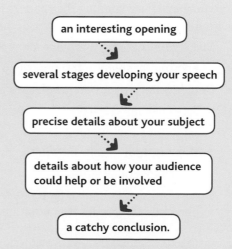

an interesting opening

several stages developing your speech

precise details about your subject

details about how your audience could help or be involved

a catchy conclusion.

Peer/Self-assessment activity

1   Check your answer to Activity 1. Did you:
  - follow the guidelines
  - plan first
  - sequence your ideas
  - have an interesting opening
  - include interesting language?

2   Now grade your answer to Activity 1 using the mark scheme below. You will need to be careful and precise in your marking. Before you do this, you might like to read extracts from two sample answers to this task on pages 86 and 87.

D
  ▶ material generally appropriately sequenced
  ▶ some evidence of structure
  ▶ clear if mechanical paragraphing
  ▶ some choice of vocabulary for effect.

C
  ▶ clear structure
  ▶ clear paragraphing
  ▶ clear choice of vocabulary for effect.

B
  ▶ well structured
  ▶ effective paragraphing with links between paragraphs
  ▶ more sophisticated vocabulary and phrasing.

- When you are writing include some of these:
  - groups of three
  - direct address to your audience using second person (you)
  - identification with your audience by using first person plural (we)
  - repetition
  - contrast
  - emotive language
  - images for effect
  - wordplay for effect.
- Think each sentence through before you write it.
- Imagine the words being read aloud.
- Make sure you are always persuading and interesting your listener.

Here are two student answers to the activities on page 84.
Write the script for a speech to be given to your school or college assembly, persuading them to support the charity of your choice.
Or
Write the script for a speech to be given to your school or college assembly, persuading them to take an interest in the sport of your choice.
Read the answers together with the examiner comments. Then check what you have learnt and try putting it into practice.

D grade answer

Student A

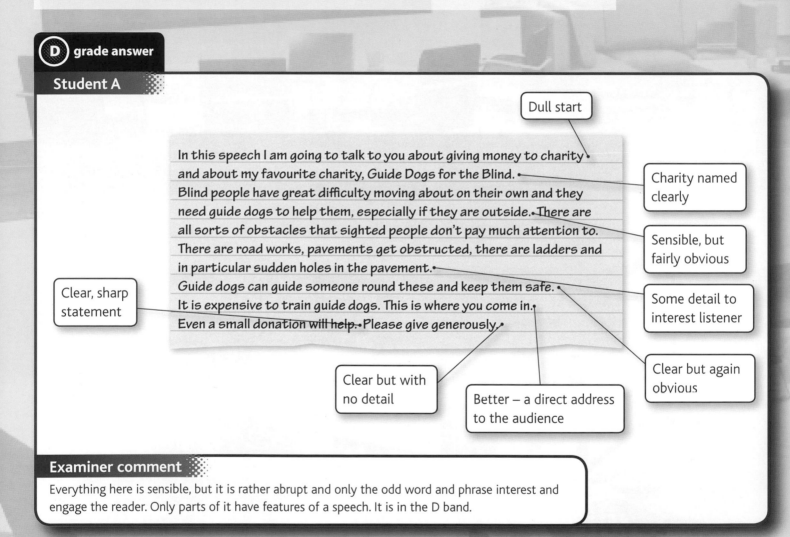

Dull start

Charity named clearly

Sensible, but fairly obvious

Some detail to interest listener

Clear, sharp statement

Clear but again obvious

Clear but with no detail

Better – a direct address to the audience

In this speech I am going to talk to you about giving money to charity and about my favourite charity, Guide Dogs for the Blind.
Blind people have great difficulty moving about on their own and they need guide dogs to help them, especially if they are outside. There are all sorts of obstacles that sighted people don't pay much attention to. There are road works, pavements get obstructed, there are ladders and in particular sudden holes in the pavement.
Guide dogs can guide someone round these and keep them safe.
It is expensive to train guide dogs. This is where you come in.
Even a small donation will help. Please give generously.

Examiner comment

Everything here is sensible, but it is rather abrupt and only the odd word and phrase interest and engage the reader. Only parts of it have features of a speech. It is in the D band.

B grade answer

Student B

Minor sentence creates more drama

Dramatic opening

Anecdote arouses interest

Link between paragraphs

List of three (a sermon technique)

> Janet is cold. And hungry. Maybe she would have been better off if she had stayed at home but after everything her step-father had done she just couldn't. Unless someone does something she will be even colder when winter comes.
>
> 'What has this to do with me?' I hear you ask.
>
> It has everything to do with you. Each of you can help young people like Janet by supporting Shelter.
>
> Shelter provides housing for the homeless. It provides food. It provides support. And people like Janet need all three.
>
> Why not resist chocolate this week and save the money for Shelter? Why not?
>
> If you don't, then people like Janet are in for a much harder time than they deserve. Please help. Give your money and time to Shelter.

Direct audience address

Tied together

Practical suggestion

Repetition of rhetorical question to challenge audience

Structure – reminds listener of opening

Direct appeal

Examiner comment

Here are many appeals to the listener with some variety of approach. There is some information, a story, some practical suggestions, rhetorical questions and an emotional appeal. The language and sentence structure is varied. The answer falls well into the B band.

Language and structure

To move up the grades, you need to:
- match your writing to purpose and audience
- think about the form of your response (the text for a speech here)
- vary your sentence structures
- vary your use of language features
- try to make the reader interested in what you write.

What have I learnt?

Discuss or jot down what you now know about:
- planning
- structuring your writing
- using language for effect.

Putting it into practice

- You can practice this skill with anything you write.
- You can get efficient at making plans.
- You can begin to sequence effectively.

My learning objectives ▶

This lesson will help you to:
● understand the different forms you need to write in
● write letters using the correct feaures.

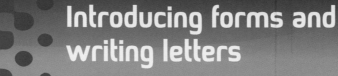

Introducing forms and writing letters

Introducing forms

We don't write everything in the same way. How we write depends very much on purpose and audience but each time we write we make choices about:

▶ form

▶ language

▶ sentence structures

▶ presentational features such as paragraphs, bullet points and headlines.

In your course you look at a wide range of forms of non-fiction and media texts. Many of these will have been to prepare for the Reading part of the exam. There are many different forms of text in the Reading section of this book. The features used in these texts are useful to you in preparing for your own writing.

Some main forms that you may be asked to write in are:

▶ reports

▶ articles

▶ letters

▶ information sheets

▶ advice sheets

▶ emails.

You may be asked to write in any two of these forms in the exam.

Letters

Remind yourself of some of the key features of letters, including:

▶ what addresses you put in

▶ where the address or addresses go

▶ the date

▶ how you start the letter (the 'salutation')

▶ how you finish the letter (the sign off).

All these will depend on the purpose of, and the audience for, the letter. On the page opposite is an example of the beginning of a formal letter written to a company.

The address of the company/person you are writing to lower down and on the left

12 Lake Street
Headingley
Leeds
LS6 3PY

Your address top right

1 December 2009

The date, beneath your address

Customer Services Manager
Moneyworks
24 Broad Street
Birmingham
B1 4RW

Dear Sir/Madam

In this instance, as the name isn't known, Dear Sir/Madam is used – the letter would end 'Yours faithfully'

If you are writing to a firm or an organisation where you don't know anybody's name you need to:

▶ put your address

▶ put the date

▶ put the address the letter is going to

▶ start with 'Dear Sir' or 'Dear Sir/Madam'

▶ sign off with 'Yours faithfully'.

Remember:

▶ if you are writing to someone whose name you know, then you start 'Dear Mr/Mrs …' and end 'Yours sincerely'

▶ if you are writing to someone who lives at the address you are sending the letter to, you don't include their address in your letter

▶ a letter to a friend would be much less formal and might start 'Dear Chris', ending with 'Love' or 'Cheers'.

Activity 1

Write the beginning and the ending of a letter to each of the following:

● a letter to a friend

● a business letter to someone whose name you don't know

● a letter replying to one from Mrs R Singh at the local tax office

● a formal letter of application for a job.

GradeStudio

Check your answer

Did you use the following correctly:

● Dear Sir/Madam, Dear Mr/Mrs, Hi mate, etc.

● Yours sincerely, Yours faithfully, Love

● your own address

● the address of the person the letter was going to

● the date?

This lesson will help you to:
- understand the features of articles, information and advice sheets
- use these features in your own writing.

Articles, information and advice sheets

Articles

When writing an article, first of all you need to decide:

▶ where it might be printed ▶ its purpose ▶ the intended audience.

Then you need to make choices about:

▶ language

▶ headings, subheadings and any other presentational features

▶ paragraphs.

Here is an example of an article which also has in it some features of an information sheet.

General introduction

Picture to make it dramatic

Article writer's name

Top heading introduces topic

Extra information about tiger sharks

Jokey headline

Open wide: Eli Martinez, carefully places food into a tiger shark's mouth on the ocean floor

The diver bringing fish suppers to one of the ocean's great predators

Grabbing a bite to eat

by **Miles Erwin**

DIVING with sharks seems crazy enough but some adrenaline junkies have taken the sport one step further by feeding the fish by hand.

Eli Martinez says there is no greater thrill than getting up close and personal with one of the most dangerous predators known to man.

'Diving with sharks is what I do,' he said. 'Some may think it's a crazy idea, but I know what I'm doing. To be with them in the ocean, swimming around, is just mind blowing.'

The retired rodeo bull rider started feeding tiger sharks without protection

two years ago, having first practised his technique on smaller species while wearing a chainmail suit.

Using bloody fish as bait, Martinez from Alamo, Texas, is able to entice the sharks amazingly close.

However, the father of four admits the sport is not without its risks after an Austrian died on an open water shark dive in the Bahamas last year.

'This was a very unfortunate accident that hopefully will never happen again,' he said.

He added: 'On several occasions, I have been chased out of the water when

the sharks have got too excited but, if you let them calm down, you can get right back in again.'

＞ Tiger shark facts

- ■ **Largest predatory shark after the Great White**
- ■ **Grows between 3.25m (10.5ft) and 4.25m (14ft) and weighs between 385kg (60st) and 900kg (142st)**
- ■ **Eats the most varied diet of any shark, including dolphins, snakes, turtles – and even tyres**
- ■ **Gets name from stripes on body which gradually fade with age**

Main character of story introduced

Direct speech for authenticity

Tabloid paragraphs each with a slightly different angle

GradeStudio

Check your answer

Did you:
- choose different headlines for each of the three
- think carefully about your audiences
- use language to interest each of your audiences?

Activity 1

Write the first two paragraphs of an article on how to make the most of your money for:

1 your school magazine

2 a tabloid newspaper

3 an article in the financial section of a broadsheet newspaper.

Information and advice sheets

These are designed to get specific information across to the reader clearly and directly. The layout of the information and advice is therefore key to the sheet's success. Such sheets often have:

▶ headings and subheadings

▶ different styles (bold, italic, capitals, underlining, print size)

▶ bullet points and other listing devices

▶ informative language for an information sheet

▶ persuasive language and conditionals (e.g. *could*, *should*, *ought to*, *must*) for an advice sheet.

Although this is a holiday advertisement, it uses the features of an information sheet in order to cram a lot of information into a short space.

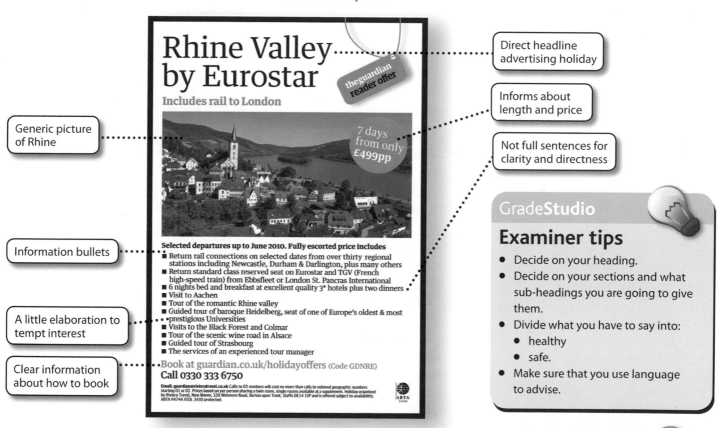

Direct headline advertising holiday

Informs about length and price

Not full sentences for clarity and directness

Generic picture of Rhine

Information bullets

A little elaboration to tempt interest

Clear information about how to book

Rhine Valley by Eurostar
Includes rail to London

theguardian reader offer

7 days from only **£499pp**

Selected departures up to June 2010. Fully escorted price includes

■ Return rail connections on selected dates from over thirty regional stations including Newcastle, Durham & Darlington, plus many others
■ Return standard class reserved seat on Eurostar and TGV (French high-speed train) from Ebbsfleet or London St. Pancras International
■ 6 nights bed and breakfast at excellent quality 3* hotels plus two dinners
■ Visit to Aachen
■ Tour of the romantic Rhine valley
■ Guided tour of baroque Heidelberg, seat of one of Europe's oldest & most prestigious Universities
■ Visits to the Black Forest and Colmar
■ Tour of the scenic wine road in Alsace
■ Guided tour of Strasbourg
■ The services of an experienced tour manager

Book at guardian.co.uk/holidayoffers (Code GDNRE)
Call 0330 333 6750

Email: guardian@rivieratravel.co.uk Calls to 03 numbers will cost no more than calls to national geographic numbers starting 01 or 02. Prices based on per person sharing a twin room, single rooms available at a supplement. Holiday organised by Riviera Travel, New Manor, 328 Wetmore Road, Burton upon Trent, Staffs DE14 1SP and is offered subject to availability. ABTA V4744 ATOL 3430 protected.

GradeStudio

Examiner tips

● Decide on your heading.
● Decide on your sections and what sub-headings you are going to give them.
● Divide what you have to say into:
  ● healthy
  ● safe.
● Make sure that you use language to advise.

Activity 2

You have been asked to produce some material about health and safety in your school or college.

1 Write an information sheet for students telling them what the issues are.

2 Write an advice sheet advising them how to keep healthy and safe while at school or college.

Include instructions to the designer on the presentational features you would like to include.

GradeStudio

Check your answer

Did you:

● think carefully about layout
● think carefully about presentation
● use sections, bullet points, underlining
● choose language to inform
● choose language to advise
● choose language suitable for your audience?

My learning ▶

This lesson will help you to:
- understand the features of reports, text messages and emails
- use these features in your own writing.

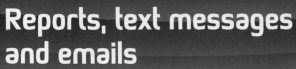

Reports, text messages and emails

Reports

In the workplace people are often asked to write reports: perhaps minutes of meetings; perhaps a briefing paper for people who have not been involved in the discussions about something that you have been; perhaps a summary of different points for action; perhaps a summary of the main issues about a topic.

These are usually written in formal Standard English and include headings and bullet points. It is a useful skill to be able to write reports.

GradeStudio

Examiner tips

Make a list of all the points you are going to include and sequence them before you begin to write. Decide:
- whether you are going to number your points
- whether you use paragraphs and, if so, what length they should be.

GradeStudio

Check your answer

- Is the information clear?
- Is it easy to follow?
- Is the format consistent?
- Do the Conclusion and Recommendations follow from what you have already included?

 Activity 1

Think about a topic that you have heard a discussion about recently and write a report which summarises the main points made for people who were not present. The main topic should have a heading and the sub-sections should have sub-headings.

For example, you might have been involved in a school council discussion about whether there should be more revision classes for GCSE. You might use this heading:

Revision classes

and these sub-headings:
- Advantages
- Disadvantages
- Possible times for classes
- Conclusion
- Recommendations.

You could use this structure and format for many different topics.

Now choose a topic and a purpose and an audience for your report and write it using the structure given above.

Text messages

Text messaging has conventions all of its own. The idea is to get the message across as quickly as possible and so abbreviations and symbols are used as well as emoticons. Text messages are usually informal, although this can vary depending on the relationship between sender and receiver.

It is perhaps the most difficult of forms to master because each writer and reader has his or her own preferred abbreviations. So the language of text messaging is very individual and it's unlikely that you will be asked to produce a text message in the exam. However, if you are a keen text messager then you should think about your own use of language (and symbols and emoticons). Is your message clear? Is it ambiguous (could it mean more than one thing)?

Informal text

Phonetic abbreviations

Symbols

Punctuation only when needed for clarity

Abbreviation when meaning clear

T.ill ⬛ ⬎ abc 18:34
New text message 981/1
To:

Message:

C u @ 8 at Via then. Lookin 4ward 2 it

Options Send Clear

Number for part of word

Slightly less informal text

Punctuation only used where useful for meaning

Grammar abbreviated

Informal salutation

Tone via punctuation

Asking for a reply

T.ill ⬛ ⬎ abc 18:34
t message 981/1

Message:

Hi have arranged so can come on Saturday! if we are still invited. X

Options Send Clear

Upper case kiss to go with 'Hi'

Punctuation at end

Emails

Informal emails also break many of the rules of Standard English. If you are emailing a friend then much of what you write may be like text messaging language, with abbreviations, symbols, missing apostrophes, few if any capital letters and mistakes uncorrected.

Email, though, is now also a primary means of business communication. Many people write dozens of emails each day but they must be certain that their message is clear and so they use many (sometimes all) of the conventions of Standard English. These formal emails are a more common means of communication than letters these days, but they obey the Standard English conventions.

A formal email often has these features:

▶ no addresses (because you are writing to a specific person and your email address and theirs is at the top)

▶ a salutation

▶ a sign off.

So a formal email is more like a letter than a text message, although it might be very brief and direct.

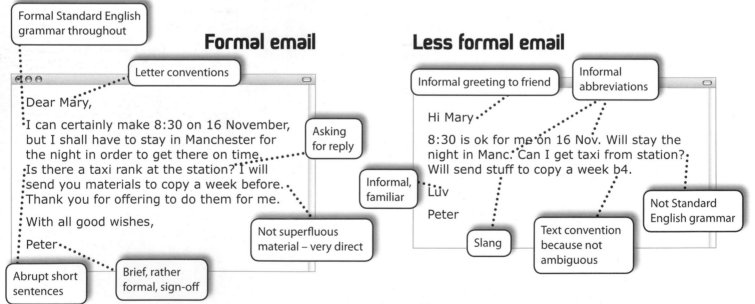

Formal email

Formal Standard English grammar throughout

Letter conventions

Dear Mary,

I can certainly make 8:30 on 16 November, but I shall have to stay in Manchester for the night in order to get there on time. Is there a taxi rank at the station? I will send you materials to copy a week before. Thank you for offering to do them for me.

With all good wishes,

Peter

Asking for reply

Not superfluous material – very direct

Abrupt short sentences

Brief, rather formal, sign-off

Less formal email

Informal greeting to friend

Informal abbreviations

Hi Mary

8:30 is ok for me on 16 Nov. Will stay the night in Manc. Can I get taxi from station? Will send stuff to copy a week b4.

Luv

Peter

Informal, familiar

Slang

Text convention because not ambiguous

Not Standard English grammar

Activity 2

Write three things, each of them with the purpose of arranging a meeting:

- a formal email to work colleagues
- an informal email to a relative
- a text message to your closest friend.

Assessment practice

My learning ▶

This lesson will help you to:
- practise your writing, focusing your information and ideas
- assess your answer by looking at other responses.

Complete the following activity and then the Peer/Self-assessment activity that follows.

Activity 1

Your local newspaper has recently published an article saying that young people nowadays spend their time vandalising the neighbourhood and terrorising older people.

Write a letter to the editor of the local newspaper expressing your own point of view.

Peer/Self-assessment activity

1. Check your answer to Activity 1.
   - Is your letter clear?
   - Did it have the right salutation and sign off?
   - Did you express your own point of view?

2. Now grade your answer to Activity 1 using the mark scheme below. You will need to be careful and precise in your marking. Before you do this, you might like to read some sample answers on this task on pages 96 and 97.

D
- ▶ some relevant material
- ▶ some appropriate tone for letter to local newspaper
- ▶ attempts to engage with activity.

C
- ▶ clear attempt to engage with activity
- ▶ several different points appropriately sequenced
- ▶ clear attempt to write a letter to local newspaper.

B
- ▶ clear and effective letter
- ▶ range of relevant points and detail
- ▶ clear understanding of topic, purpose and audience.

GradeStudio

Here are two student answers to the activity on page 95.
Write a letter to the editor of the local newspaper expressing your own point of view.
Read the answers together with the examiner comments. Then check what you have learnt and try putting it into practice.

C grade answer

Student C

Correct salutation

Dear Sir,

You published a letter last week from Mr Reece-Johnson about young people being a scary nuisance. Some young people may be but we are not all.

Introduces topic and gives view

We go about together because we have friends. We hang around bus stops because we use public transport. We are in groups about 3.30 because that is when we finish school.

Addresses three issues in letter succinctly

Most young people care about their futures and work hard at school and with their homework. Many young people visit and look after older people.

Response to issues

Mr Reece-Johnson should not dismiss all young people on the basis of a bad experience with one or two.

Yours faithfully,

Peter Green

Suitable conclusion

Correct sign off

Examiner comment

This is a clear letter, correctly set out and expressing the writer's views. The four brief paragraphs each mark a stage in the letter. There is some information, points from the original letter are addressed and the tone is appropriate. It is clearly in the C band.

D grade answer

Student B

Correct salutation

Introduces the topic

Dear Sir,

I don't agree with Mr Reece-Johnson that young people are a nuisance. They do their best. Just because old people don't like our clothes doesn't make us bad. And groups of old people standing together, pushing to get on the bus before us are just as frightening to us.

Mr Reece-Johnson should learn some respect. He can't go around calling us names all the time. He should mind his own business and get on with his life rather than making accusations about us young people.

I hope you will print this letter in your newspaper.

Yours sincerely,

Jemma Princeton

Appropriate paragraph

Own view, though a bit confrontational

Too aggressive and not really showing point of view about topic

Not necessary

Wrong sign off (it should be 'Yours faithfully')

Examiner comment

The salutation is correct and the two paragraphs are appropriate but the sign off is wrong. There is very little material here. Few individual points from the original letter are picked up. The tone is too confrontational. It is an attempt but not a very successful one. It is in the D band.

Use and adapt forms

To move up the grades, make sure you include the correct addresses for the kind of letter you are writing. Make sure you match the salutation and the sign off correctly. Use your paragraphs properly and try to make some links between paragraphs. Try to match your tone to the purpose and audience of your text.

What have I learnt?

Discuss or jot down what you now know about:
• planning
• sequencing
• using the correct form
• checking your work.

Putting it into practice

• You can practise this skill with anything you write.
• Make plans.
• Sequence your ideas.
• Think about paragraphs and links between paragraphs.

Use accurate punctuation

My learning ▶

This lesson will help you to:
- gain an overview of punctuation
- understand how to use commas, full stops and capital letters.

Commas, full stops and capital letters

GradeStudio

Examiner tip

- When it comes to writing tasks in the exam, it's so important to work out what you are going to say first. This way you can concentrate on **how** you are writing.

Introduction to punctuation

To help you use accurate punctuation you should know that:

▶ a full stop, question mark or exclamation mark comes at the end of every sentence: •

▶ question marks come at the end of every question: **?**

▶ exclamation marks come after an exclamation: **!**

▶ what people say, and book titles, are in inverted commas: **' '**

▶ commas separate items in a list or denote a pause in the sentence, usually where there is a subordinating clause, or act in pairs instead of brackets: **,**

▶ a colon introduces a list: **:**

▶ a semi-colon separates full sentences which are closely interrelated and interdependent in meaning: **;**

Commas, full stops and capital letters

It's rare to find students who don't know where to put full stops, commas and capital letters. Most mistakes that are made in the exam are when they are concentrating on what they are saying rather than how they are saying it.

Read the following passage to see how it illustrates the rules which appear around the text.

1 Each new sentence starts with a capital letter.

2 Capital letters are also used for names.

3 Capital letters are used for the main words in titles

4 Each sentence ends with a full stop (or question mark or exclamation mark).

5 Commas separate items in a list except for the last two which are joined by 'and'.

6 A comma is used after 'however' if it starts a sentence.

7 Commas in pairs separate off from the rest of the sentence something which could have been put in brackets.

8 A comma sometimes denotes a pause in the sentence, usually before a new clause is introduced.

Accurate punctuation helps the reader to follow what is being said. Lynn Truss made this clear in her book 'Eats Shoots and Leaves'. She showed how inaccurate punctuation confuses the reader, creates ambiguities and is a sign of sloppy thinking. However, clear and accurate punctuation makes reading easy. Pairs of commas, showing that items placed between them are separate from the rest of the sentence, help the reader to keep the main point in mind. Although Lynn Truss's book is actually a serious book about accuracy in writing, she makes it amusing to read.

Look at the sentences below. They are all taken from a newspaper article entitled 'Need an Autumn Break?'. Now look again at the rules in the example opposite. Which of these rules are being followed in the 11 sentences below? The first one is done for you.

1 Travel, as any philosopher or fool will tell you, is what you make of it.
   Rules 1, 4 and 7.

2 You could be sitting in an aluminium box, eight miles above the Arctic circle, squabbling with your partner.

3 You could be herded through the Alhambra, the Louvre or Machu Picchu so quickly and in such a vast crowd that you feel you've scarcely seen it.

4 Or you can stop, think about what it means to travel and just start looking outside your front door.

5 Here's a little test for you.

6 Can you name the nearest Area of Outstanding Natural Beauty to your house?

7 What about the nearest forest?

8 Or the nearest house?

9 The nearest canal?

10 There you go.

11 That's the next few weekends sorted.

The full stops and capital letters have been omitted from the opening of the following newspaper article.

Write the passage out correctly, putting the full stops and capital letters in the right places.

You can't go anywhere in manchester at the moment the tram tracks are all up in the city centre and it's chaos you can't even get a bus to the tram either if you want to go to the lowry centre in salford quays you have to go to st peter's square and hope a tram will come someone told me the other day that it was about water pipes but i haven't seen anything about it in the press and there aren't any posters about it maybe the council thinks visitors don't count

GradeStudio

Check your answer

Did you put in:
● six full stops
● 14 capital letters
Are they all now in the right places?

My learning ▶

This lesson will help you to:
- understand how to use apostrophes
- understand how to use question marks and exclamations.

Apostrophes, question marks and exclamations

Apostrophes

Apostrophes are used in two cases.

▶ They show that a letter is missing, e.g. *can't* (short for *cannot*).

▶ They show possession, e.g. *Janet's* (meaning 'belonging to Janet').

Missing letters

Activity 1

1 Find and copy out the examples of apostrophes to show missing letters in the following passage.

2 Write out the words that would be there if the apostrophe was not being used. For example: *I'm = I am*.

> I can't help but think that I'm going to improve my punctuation skills by concentrating hard on it. In fact we're all going to improve. That's because we're going to be thinking about detail and because we know that we can't afford to make too many mistakes. It's not hard, really.

Possession

The rules here are quite straightforward.

▶ If it belongs to something singular, then write the word, add the apostrophe and add an 's'. For example:

  ▶ *the pig's trotters* – the trotters belonging to one pig
  ▶ *your heart's desire* – the desire belonging to your heart
  ▶ *the class's classroom* – the classroom belonging to one class.

▶ If it belongs to something plural ending in 's', then write the word and add an apostrophe. For example:

  ▶ *the pigs' trotters* – the trotters belonging to more than one pig
  ▶ *their hearts' desires* – the desires belonging to their hearts
  ▶ *the classes' classroom* – the classroom belonging to more than one class.

▶ If, however, it belongs to something plural which doesn't end in an 's', then write the word, add an apostrophe and add an 's'. For example:

  ▶ *the children's books*
  ▶ *the sheep's pasture.*

The only exception to these rules covers a class of words called possessives.

▶ These words carry the idea of possession inside them and so they don't have an apostrophe. Here they are:

  ▶ *yours, his, hers, its, theirs, ours.*

If you follow these simple rules then you can't go wrong with apostrophes.

▶ Remember, however:

  ▶ *its* means 'belonging to it'
  ▶ *it's* means 'it is'.

Activity 2

Just to check that you have got the idea, put the apostrophes in the right places when they are needed in the following examples.

1 Its not enough just to write your answer.

2 Youve got to make sure that you check carefully.

3 Students errors often lead to their underperformance.

4 Almost every piece of work in the exam has its errors.

5 The twins faces were identical.

Question marks and exclamation marks

Remember:

▶ a question mark is needed at the end of every direct question

▶ an exclamation is a shout, so use an exclamation mark when something is shouted or when something is a shock or surprise.

Direct questions are those which are asking a question. For example:

Where are you going? or *Why are exams necessary?*

Some students tend to overuse exclamation marks. One is plenty. Don't decorate the page by doubling or trebling them. If you think about the 'shout', then you will be safe. For example:

Then I fell asleep doesn't need an exclamation mark but *Ouch!* does.

Activity 3

Read the following rather informal text and put in the question marks and exclamation marks, as well as the full stops and capital letters.

Women playing football do you think this is a cool idea ridiculous women should know their place and not mess with men's sports that's the view of lots of men who don't know how good women can be at football which arsenal team won this year's championship was it the men no way the women which national team made it to the finals of the Euros this year

GradeStudio

Check your answer

Did you put in:

● two (or possibly three) full stops

● four question marks

● two (or possibly three) exclamation marks?

Are they all now in the right places?

My learning ▶

This lesson will help you to:
- understand how to use colons and semi-colons
- understand how to use inverted commas.

Colons, semi-colons and inverted commas

Colons

The **colon** is used:

▶ to introduce a list. For example:

 ▶ *If you go camping you will need: a tent, a sleeping bag, a torch and warm clothes.*

▶ to introduce quoted direct speech. For example:

 ▶ *A lady on the bus shouted after me: 'You have forgotten your bag!'*

You should be very confident about using colons if you have read much of this book. There are hundreds of them because there are lots of lists. Most of these lists, though, are in bullet point form. They could have been written in continuous prose instead, in which case the colon would have introduced the list and then the items would have been separated out by commas except for the last two which would have been linked by 'and'.

Semi-colons

The **semi-colon** is used in two cases:

▶ where two full sentences are very closely linked together. For example:

 ▶ *I love eating spaghetti bolognaise; it is my favourite meal.*

▶ where a colon has introduced a list and the items in the list are grammatically full sentences. When this is the case these items in the list are separated by semi-colons rather than commas. For example:

 ▶ *I have lots to do in town: I need to buy a dress; I have to meet my friend; I must post a letter.*

Activity 1

Here are two sentences that need colons and semi-colons. Decide whether a colon or a semi-colon should go in each place indicated by a number.

1 There were many sides to William Shakespeare (1) actor, playwright, husband, father and property owner.

2 There were many sides to William Shakespeare (1) he was an actor (2) he wrote plays (3) he was a husband and father and he was a property owner.

Inverted commas

These are used in two situations:

▶ around direct speech

▶ around titles of books, films, short stories, plays or poems (except for the Bible and the Koran).

All direct speech (a quotation of what exactly someone said) has to have inverted commas round it. But when you are writing dialogue, remember that each new speaker must be in a new paragraph.

The following extract from Doris Lessing's 'Flight' shows speech set out correctly.

He stumped his feet alternately, thump, thump, on the wooden floor and shouted: 'She'll marry him. I'm telling you, she'll be marrying him next!'

His daughter rose swiftly, brought him a cup, set him a plate.

'Now, now,' she crooned. 'What's wrong with him? Why not?'

Activity 2

Below is a piece of conversation with the inverted commas missing. Write it out putting the inverted commas in the right places.

Remember:

● each new speaker needs to be in a new paragraph

● speech needs inverted commas round it

● book, film, short story or play titles need inverted commas round them.

What are you reading? Mark asked. I'm reading that book by Lance Armstrong about winning the Tour de France. What's it called? It's called Every Second Counts, I think.

This lesson will help you to:
- practise your writing focusing on your use of punctuation
- assess your answer by looking at other responses.

Assessment practice

Now you are going to have a go at an exam style question. Attempt the activity in the time suggested and then complete the Peer/Self-assessment activity that follows.

Activity 1

Write for 10 minutes on the following activity, making sure that you use a range of punctuation correctly:

Persuade the reader that it would be a good thing if everyone became a vegetarian.

Peer/Self-assessment activity

1 Check your answer to Activity 1. Did you:
- include a range of punctuation
- check all your full stops
- check your commas, question marks and exclamation marks
- check any other items of punctuation?

2 Now grade the punctuation in your answer to Activity 1 using the mark scheme below. You will need to be precise and careful in your marking. Before you do this, you might like to read some sample answers on this activity on page 105.

D ▶ uses a range of punctuation.

C ▶ generally accurate punctuation.

B ▶ largely accurate punctuation
▶ effective range of punctuation used correctly.

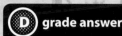

GradeStudio

Here are two student answers to the activity on page 104.
Persuade the reader that it would be a good thing if everyone became a vegetarian.
Read the answers together with the examiner comments. Then check what you have learnt and try putting it into practice.

D grade answer

Student A

> **Comma used instead of full stop**
>
> **Comma used instead of full stop**

People would be much healthier if they were vegetarians, they wouldn't have so much heart-attack inducing cholesterol and they would smell better. Animals would be better off too, they could live happy and contented lives without having to worry about being eaten. How would you like to be bred to be eaten. How would you like to be fattened up for slaughter. You wouldn't! None of us would be worse off if we did without beef, pork, lamb and chicken.

> **Question mark missing**
>
> **Question mark missing**

Examiner comment

There is a range of punctuation here used correctly: commas in lists, an exclamation mark and three full stops. There are two occasions, though when a comma is used instead of a full stop. If there were only one, then the punctuation could be said to be 'generally accurate', but two suggests that the student is uncertain about when to use a full stop. Two question marks are also missing. The answer falls in the D range.

B grade answer

Student B

> **Apostrophe missing**

Would you like to be fattened up for slaughter before being butchered? Of course you wouldn't. Still less would you like to be fattened up and eaten? So why do so many people think animals can be treated like this? Is it because they're hypocrites? Is it because they think animals don't matter as much as people? Theres something wrong with people who think an animal doesn't have the right to a decent life.

Examiner comment

There is only one punctuation error here, so the answer can be considered to be generally accurate. This apart, the punctuation is used effectively. The punctuation in this answer falls in the B band.

Punctuation

To move up the grades, you need to be able to:
- read what you have just written very carefully
- check all your full stops
- find and correct any errors
- make sure you haven't been inconsistent with your spelling.

What have I learnt?

Discuss or jot down what you now know about:
- using a range of punctuation
- using punctuation marks accurately
- what the examiners are looking for.

Putting it into practice

- You can practise this skill with anything you write.
- You can notice how punctuation is used in a wide range of texts.
- You can practise checking your own punctuation in everything you write.

My learning ▶

This lesson will help you to:
- spell as accurately as you can
- identify errors you often make.

Identifying and correcting spelling errors

Many students think that it's their teacher's job to find their spelling mistakes for them. It isn't. It's your job. You haven't got your teacher with you in the exam room, so you need to get lots of practice in finding your mistakes and correcting them. Checking your work for spelling in the writing tasks is really important in the exam.

It's usually much easier to find errors in something someone else has written than it is to find them in something that you have written. If you are looking at something you have just written then you are tempted to see what you ought to have written rather than what you have actually written.

The way people learn to spell is very individual. There's no quick and easy way to spell everything correctly; it needs some hard work over a period of time.

The best thing to do is to keep a spelling notebook where you write down the correct spelling of all words you often spell wrongly. You can identify these from all your GCSE subjects.

You should:

▶ write down the words you misspell

▶ look up the correct spellings in a dictionary

▶ learn the correct spelling of words you often misspell.

GradeStudio

Examiner tip

- It is crucial that you leave enough time in the exam to check your written work. Poor spelling can lose you vital marks.

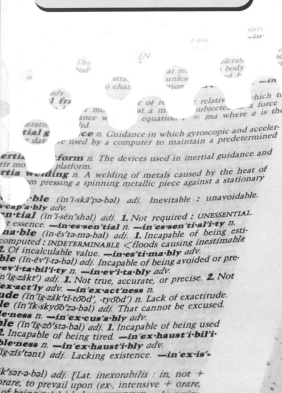

Activity 1

Find the errors in this letter written by a student to a newspaper. Look up the spellings in a dictionary and write out the correct spellings. If you are using a spelling notebook, and you didn't know how to spell these words, add them to your notebook.

Dear Editor,

I am writing to complain about an artical in your newspaper last week. Your reportor said that children should not be allowed to take part in talent compatitions in televsion becaus they might get upset if they made a mistake and this then upset the viewers.

I don't agree with this. Talant is talant and it doesn't matter how old the person is. After all, adults might get upset, too, if they mess up. Thier lives are affected, too. Some children are brillyant at doing things and they ought to be given a chance to show of what they can do.

Your reported shouldn't of taken this view becaus it discrimminates against children who mite be just as talented as adults. I think most television viewers will agree with me.

Yours sincerly,

A Student

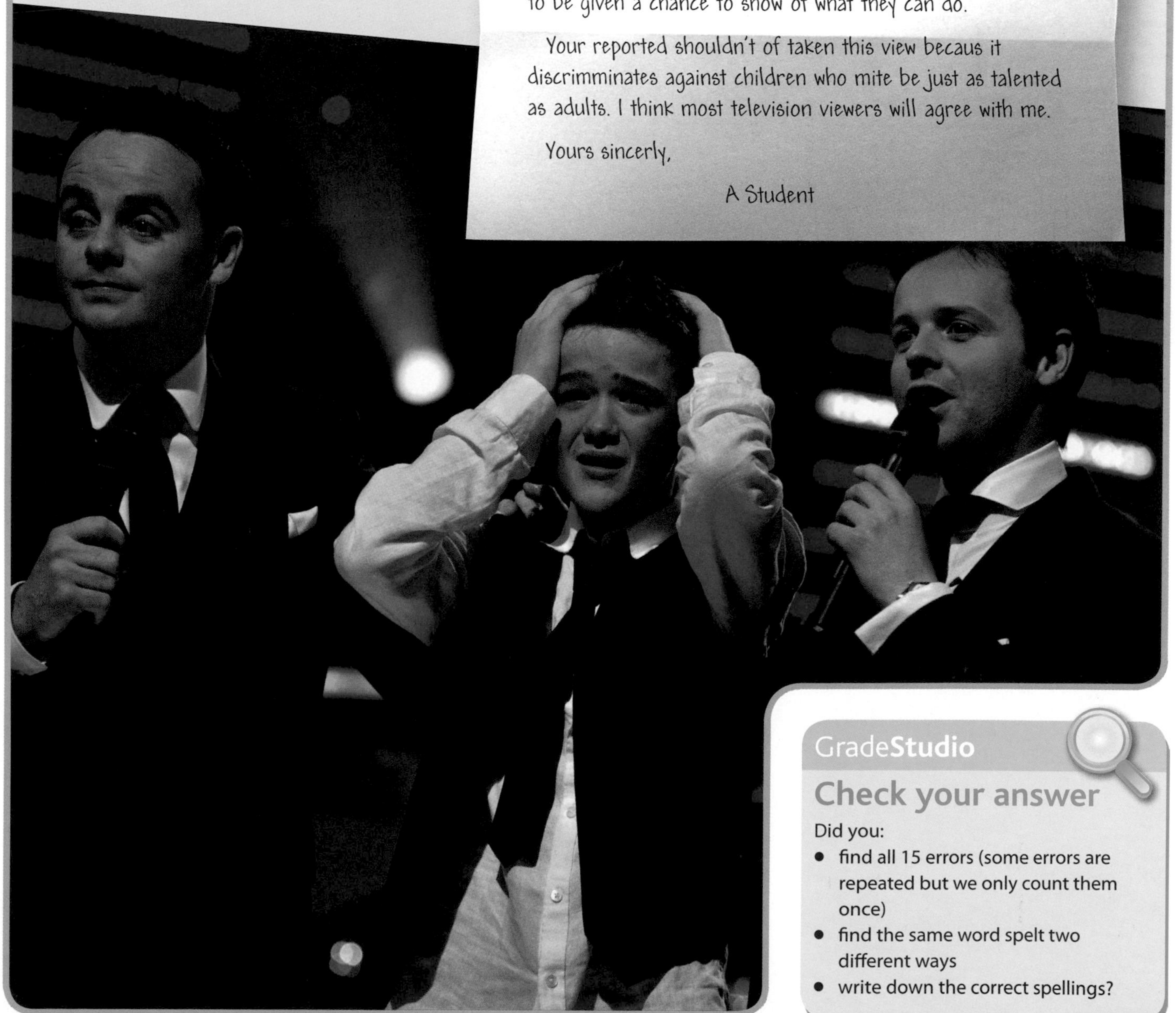

GradeStudio

Check your answer

Did you:

- find all 15 errors (some errors are repeated but we only count them once)
- find the same word spelt two different ways
- write down the correct spellings?

This lesson will help you to:
● practise your writing focusing on your spelling
● assess your answer by looking at other responses.

Assessment practice

Complete the following activity and then the Peer/Self-assessment activity that follows.

Activity 1

Spend about 10 minutes writing your own text.

Choose something you know a lot about – whether it is sport, gardening, reading or something entirely different – and explain why you are interested in it.

Use as wide a range of interesting words as you can.

When you have finished:

● look carefully at the spellings
● use a dictionary to correct any words you have misspelt
● use a dictionary to check any words you are unsure about.

GradeStudio

Examiner tip

● In the exam most spelling errors are what examiners would call 'careless mistakes'. The student knows very well how to spell the words but is thinking about what to write rather than concentrating on what he or she is writing. This is why, when it comes to the writing tasks in the exam, it's so important to work out what you are going to say first so that when you are writing you can concentrate on **how** you are writing.

Peer/Self-assessment activity

1 Check your answer to Activity 1. Did you:
  • find your spelling errors
  • use a dictionary
  • add any words to your spelling notebook?

2 Now grade the spelling in your answer to Activity 1 using the mark scheme below. You will need to be careful and precise in your marking. Before you do this you might like to read some sample answers on this activity on page 109.

D ▶ some accurate spelling of more complex words.

C ▶ generally accurate spelling.

B ▶ generally accurate spelling of commonly used words and of several more complex words.

GradeStudio

Here are two student answers to the activity on page 108.
Choose something you know a lot about and explain why you are interested in it.
Read the answers together with the examiner comments. Then check what you have learnt and try putting it into practice.

(D) grade answer

Student A

One word, not two

Error

'there' and 'their' confused

Error

Error – careless

Cooking is fun. You can make almost anything you want and lots of things
are quick to make. Ingreadients are their in the cuboard waiting to
be turned in to a tasty dish. You can use a recipe book to tell you wot
order to do things in if you cant remeber. Cooking can give you alot of
satisfaction.

Two words, not one

Correct – more complex word

Apostrophe missing

Careless error – letter missing

Correct – more complex word

Examiner comment

Although there are careless errors here as well as mistakes, two complex words are spelt correctly and so the answer is in the D band.

(C) grade answer

Student B

'its' and 'it's' confused

I am interested in gardening because its fun to grow your own food and its
much cheaper than buying all your stuff at the shop. Even small children
can enjoy gardening because things like lettuces and radishes will grow
almost anywhere and they grow very quickly. Although you have to keep a
watch on your crops its nice to come home and check how everything is
doing and you can eat things you have grown when they are ready.

'its' and 'it's' confused again

Examiner comment

The spelling here is generally accurate, although the vocabulary is simple and there are few complex words. 'Interested' and 'gardening' are spelt correctly. So are 'lettuces' and 'although'. So even though the vocabulary is not very ambitious there are some complex words spelt correctly. The spelling falls into the C band.

Spelling

To move up the grades, you need to be able to:
- read what you have just written very carefully
- find and correct any errors you have made
- make sure you haven't spelt the same word in different ways.

What have I learnt?

Discuss or jot down what you now know about:
- finding spelling errors
- using a dictionary
- checking your work.

Putting it into practice

- You can practise this skill with anything you write.
- Keep using a dictionary.
- Keep adding words to your spelling notebook.
- Learn the correct spelling of words in your notebook.

109

My learning ▶

This lesson will help you to:
- write sentences accurately
- use a range of sentence structures and sentence forms for effect.

Sentence structures

Simple, compound and complex sentences

The simplest definition of a sentence is that it has to contain a subject and main verb ('doing' or 'state of mind' word). Here is a reminder of the main types of sentence structures.

▶ A **simple sentence** has a subject and a main verb. For example:

> subject   verb
>
> *I feel happy.*

▶ A **compound sentence** is a series of simple sentences joined together (usually with 'and' or 'but'). For example:

> conjunction
>
> *I feel happy and I am doing well at school.*

▶ A **complex sentence** is often longer, with one part dependent on another (using words like 'because', 'although', 'until'). For example:

> subordinating conjunction
>
> *I feel happy because I am doing well at school.*

Activity 1

Read the following sentences which are about tennis. Decide which kind of sentence (simple, compound or complex) each of the following is.

1 Loud grunting is a feature of modern professional tennis.
2 Monica Seles was one of the first loud grunters.
3 Although grunting is fashionable, some of the best players don't grunt.
4 Maria Sharapova is a very loud grunter and her grunts sound more like screams.
5 Before grunting became fashionable it was thought to be unsporting.
6 The public ought to boo grunters and referees should disqualify them.

QUIET PLEASE... THE PLAYERS ARE ABOUT TO BEGIN GRUNTING

GradeStudio

Check your answer

- Did you find two examples of each of the three types of sentences?

Minor sentences

In addition to these three types of sentences, writers sometimes use a sentence that doesn't have a verb in it. This is called a minor sentence and is usually used for a dramatic effect or a jolt to the reader because it comes after some much longer sentences. For example:

'Gutted!' is the minor sentence in this text.

> I had queued all night for Centre Court tickets at Wimbledon, but when I got to the front of the queue I found that the last one had been sold. Gutted!

Examiner advice about sentence structures

▶ Writing that is going to interest and engage the reader will have a variety of sentence structures. This is what examiners are looking for in the exam. The examiner is also hoping that you will use what is called 'sentence forms for effect'. This means that you are choosing to construct your sentence in a particular way because you know it will have an effect on the reader. The use of the minor sentence *'Gutted!'* (above) is a good example of this.

▶ Every sentence ends in a full stop – or in its equivalent, a question mark or an exclamation mark. The most common mistake that students make in the exam is to put a comma where there should be a full stop. Examiners call these 'comma splices' and they don't like them. Think through what you are going to write in your sentence before you begin to write it.

▶ Try to get used to thinking in sentence units. This will make sure you put the full stop in the right place when the sentence ends.

GradeStudio

Examiner tip

- Don't use minor sentences too often and make sure they are for a particular effect.

Activity 2

Find and correct the comma splices (for a definition see the Examiner advice above) in the following piece of writing.

> There are twenty thousand islands in the South Pacific, they were created by the lava thrown up by powerful volcanoes under the sea. Coral reefs are eventually formed and the sea around these atolls is teeming with life. Hawaii is the most famous place created by these underwater volcanoes, land is being created there all the time. Some trees are attracted to the lava and when they start to grow exotic birds come to feed off the fruit of the trees.

> Underground are enormous lava tubes, these are formed by the flows of lava but when the lava stops flowing these holes are left. There are all kinds of strange creatures living there, most, like spiders, crickets and translucent earwigs, have lost all their colour because they live in total darkness. The weirdly named small-eyed big-eyed hunting spider is the strangest. Totally blind, despite its name, it preys on other smaller creatures by sensing their whereabouts.

This lesson will help you to:
● practise your writing and identify sentence structures
● assess your answer by looking at other responses.

Assessment practice

Complete the following activity and then the Peer/Self-assessment activity that follows.

Activity 1

Write for 10 minutes on the following activity:

Imagine you are daydreaming in a classroom with a window. Describe what you can see outside the window.

Concentrate on creating a variety of sentence structures.

Peer/Self-assessment activity

1 When you have finished your answer to Activity 1, identify the kinds of sentences you or a partner have used. Annotate your answer to identify examples of the following:
● simple sentence
● compound sentence
● complex sentence
● minor sentence
● using sentence forms for effect.

Rewrite what you did if your piece does not contain all five of the above.

2 Now grade your answer to Activity 1 using the mark scheme below. You will need to be careful and precise in your marking. Before you do this, you might like to read some sample answers on this activity on page 113.

D

▶ uses some kinds of sentence structures
▶ the majority of sentences securely marked out.

C

▶ uses a range of sentence structures (at least three kinds)
▶ an example of a sentence form for effect
▶ sentences generally accurately marked out.

B

▶ uses range of sentence forms for effect
▶ sentences accurately marked out.

GradeStudio

Here are two student answers to the activity on page 112.

Imagine you are daydreaming in a classroom with a window. Describe what you can see outside the window.

Read the answers together with the examiner comments. Then check what you have learnt and try putting it into practice.

D grade answer

Student A

> Outside I can see a large tree with lots of leaves. It hasn't lost its leaves yet. In the distance are some sheep. They make the landscape look dotted with white. If you went up to them they wouldn't be white, though. They would be grey, made dirty by the grime left over from the winter. I can also see some goalposts. No one is playing football yet because it's still the morning. Everyone is still inside.

Complex sentence

Complex sentence

Examiner comment

The sentences are accurately marked out here. There is a full stop at the end of every sentence, but there are only two kinds of sentence – simple and complex. There is not enough range of sentence structure here to go higher than a D.

B grade answer

Student B

Complex sentence

Minor sentence: sentence form for effect

Simple sentence

> Outside, the tree. It's still wearing all its leaves because autumn is not quite here yet. I wish I were outside. Sheep in the distance dot the landscape with white and chase each other, playing, unlike the kids trapped inside, leaving the goalposts on the playing field deserted. Oh to be free!

Complex sentence

Minor sentence: sentence form for effect

Examiner comment

There are three different kinds of sentence here, all securely and accurately marked out. The answer falls in the B band.

Sentence structure

To move up the grades, you need to be able to:
- vary your sentence structures
- think in terms of sentence units while you are writing.

What have I learnt?

Discuss or jot down what you now know about:
- different sentence structures
- how to use them effectively
- using sentence forms for effect
- where to put full stops
- what the examiners are looking for.

Putting it into practice

- You can practise this skill with anything you write.

Section C
Studying spoken language

If you are taking GCSE English Language, you will study spoken language. Spoken language is the basis for so much of our communication – rarely in your whole life will a day pass without you actually speaking to someone. How you and others use speech, and how speech varies according to different circumstances, can help you to think about what you want to say to people, and what they are saying to you.

How will I be assessed?

Your work will be assessed through one written assignment of between 800–1000 words, which must be written under controlled conditions. You do not necessarily have to write a traditional essay in this assignment, although you are certainly allowed to do so. Instead, though, you could possibly write in forms such as:

▶ a report (similar perhaps to the way you write in science)

▶ a piece of journalism

▶ a review

▶ any other form, so long as it suits the purpose of your assignment.

What will I be assessed on?

This piece of work will count for 10% of your overall marks for GCSE English Language. Your work will be assessed on the following two Assessment Objectives.

▶ Understand variations in spoken language, explaining why language changes in relation to contexts.

▶ Evaluate the impact of spoken language choices in your own and others' use.

This Assessment Objective is asking you to look at how and why peoples' spoken language might alter in relation to various factors – for example, who they are speaking to, where, and for what purpose.

This Assessment Objective is asking you to look at the potential responses people can make to the way you and others talk in any given situation.

What do spoken language tasks look like?

There are three broad areas of Spoken Language Study which you could write about. These are outlined below. For your assignment you have to choose – with the help of your teacher – one of the three areas to investigate and write about. However, you could study all three before you decide which one to focus on.

Social attitudes to spoken language

In this area you should consider the ways in which your own and others' talk is used and judged. For example, these are just some of the things you could look at:

▶ your own language use now and how it varies depending on different situations – for example, how your language changes when speaking to different people (such as your friends as opposed to your parents)

▶ how speech can give you the sense of belonging to a group – for example a regional group, an age group, an interest group, or an ethnic group (note that this unit is not just about spoken English, it is about spoken language in general. This means that you can talk about speaking other languages too)

▶ how speech is an area of public interest – for example how local speech can sometimes be ridiculed and sometimes celebrated.

Spoken genres

By genres we mean types of speech such as interviews, news reports, school assemblies and so on. So in this area you could investigate genres such as:

▶ genres you might come across in everyday life, such as school assemblies, lessons, workplace briefings

▶ media genres such as interviews, news reports, weather forecasts

▶ TV drama genres where spoken language is 'represented' – such as in soap operas, hospital dramas, crime shows, 'reality' shows and so on.

Multi-modal talk

You might think that talk is talk and writing is writing, but in recent years new genres have emerged which have elements of both. Many of these genres come from new technology, but lots of communication these days has a conversational feel to it. In this area you might look at things like:

▶ text messaging and some of its methods and rules

▶ instant messaging

▶ the use of social networking sites

▶ news stories about the use of such new technology.

My learning ▶

This lesson will help you to:
- gather your own data
- analyse and evaluate data on spoken language.

Investigating data

What is data?

Data is a word used in science as much as in English. It is information and evidence that is collected so that it can be examined, and then conclusions drawn from it. For the Spoken Language Study you will need to be able to gather and analyse data. There are many types of data you could collect and many ways to collect it. Here are some ideas:

▶ make a recording of people talking

▶ make a recording and then transcribe part of it

▶ conduct a questionnaire and/or survey

▶ collect newspaper or magazine articles

▶ use digital data from your phone, such as a text message conversation

▶ print out a chatlog or a screenshot from your computer.

Making your own recordings

Recording live conversation can open up all sorts of interesting options for your assignment. It is best to record a conversation that has some shape and purpose to it, and which has a clear context. For example, a family discussion round a table, a seated conversation about a current debate, an interview and a classroom-based discussion should all provide useful data if recorded.

You can also simply record a television or radio programme, and then choose a specific part to focus on.

GradeStudio

Examiner tip

- Ideally you will use original data for your spoken language assignment – data that you have collected yourself. Collecting good original data will improve your chances of gaining a higher mark.

GradeStudio

Examiner tips

If making your own recording of live conversation:
- Don't try to involve too many people in the conversation.
- Check that all equipment is working before you start.
- Get permission from the people taking part – you cannot secretly record people as it is against the law!
- Once you have collected a good piece of data, make sure that you copy it, and keep the copy in a safe place.

Activity 1

Try making your own recording now as a trial run. For example, you could record a class debate or a family discussion. Make sure you follow all of the Examiner tips opposite when carrying out your recording.

Making a transcript

A transcript is a written down version of the talk you have recorded. Once you have made a recording, you need to be able to use it to analyse the talk involved. For this reason, it can be very useful to have transcribed the talk.

Transcriptions often include keys or symbols just like a map does. These help the reader understand what happened in the conversation – for example, any pauses in the speech or overlaps (when people speak at the same time). There are no strict rules to these keys - the main thing is to make your key clear and easy to use by another person.

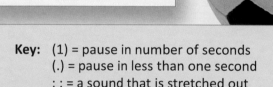

Activity 2

Below is an extract from an interview with the England football manager Fabio Capello after England had lost 1–0 in a friendly against Brazil. This was how the interview was reported in a written account of the game.

> England manager Fabio Capello said 'We played the best team in the world. Still, I learned some things. I understand the value of some players against this sort of team better now – but I will not single out players.'

1 Now look at the transcript opposite which shows what was actually said in the interview. What are the main differences between the two versions? Before you answer this, consider the following:

  a Try reading both versions aloud. What do you notice about the difference in how the two flow?

  b Do you think English is Fabio Capello's first language?

  c Why do you think Capello uses pauses and other fillers (words or sounds to fill some time), such as 'I::::::' and 'erm'?

Key: (1) = pause in number of seconds
(.) = pause in less than one second
: : = a sound that is stretched out

Interviewer: Fabio you'll be disappointed with the scoreline (.) what about the performance

Capello: yes (1) i::: we played against Brazil erm they was the best eleven for Brazil (2) the players that played the first alf was good enough

Interviewer: because you were missing so many players (1) so many senior players this evening (.) what were you actually expecting from the team that you played

(Italian translation of question heard in background)

Capello: no no no yes yes (1) for me for me it is it was interesting to er see the value of er:: to check the performance of some players (.) and I happy because some players play erm:: very well and for the future will be good for me

Interviewer: who caught your eye

(Italian translation of question heard in background)

Capello: no (1) no no I no er I not speak about one single player

Read the paragraph below, which provides you with some further context about Fabio Capello.

Fabio Capello is a highly successful football manager, who now manages the England team. An Italian, he spoke virtually no English until taking over the team two years previously. In addition to speaking English, here he is under the added pressure of responding to a defeat, and of not wanting to identify players who played poorly.

Now look in more detail at the transcript on page 117 and write an analysis of it. Consider the following questions when writing your analysis.

1 Look at what the interviewer says. What do you notice about the questions he asks and how he asks them?

2 What are the main features of the way in which Capello speaks?

3 Thinking of the overall context you have been given here, how does Capello show a lot of skill in this interview? Think about whether he actually answers the questions being asked.

To help you answer these questions, here is a response to question 1 that might give you some ideas. The Check your answer box below should help with questions 2 and 3.

Grade**Studio**

Check your answer

Look at your answer to question 2.
- Did you notice Capello's use of fillers such as 'erm' and repetition?
- Did you notice the use of some non-standard expressions, such as 'I happy' and 'They was'?
- Did you pick up on Capello's Italian accent from reading the transcript, even though there is no sound recording?

Look at your answer to question 3.
- Did you notice how Capello manages to make defeat sound quite positive?
- Did you pick up on how Capello does not really answer the questions?
- Did you think about how, perhaps because of his 'performance' of being a second language speaker, he is not given a hard time by the interviewer in the way many managers are?

The interviewer does two things before he even asks a question. First he addresses Capello by his first name, Fabio, and then he makes a statement rather than asking a question. He assumes, probably fairly, that Capello will be disappointed to lose when he says 'you'll be disappointed with the scoreline'. This helps the interviewer to establish his own presence in the conversation and to be seen as an equal, even though Capello is actually far more important.

His second question is carefully and clearly worded, but again contains an assumption, perhaps this time that Capello expected to lose.

The final question is frequently asked of managers, trying to get them to name individual players who played well or badly, but the metaphor 'caught your eye' is much more difficult for a second language speaker than the plain language used in the second question.

Here are two student answers to the activity on page 118. Read the answers together with the examiner comments.

D grade answer

Student A

> This transcript shows someone struggling to maintain an interview with a journalist even though he does not speak English very well. With the help of an interpreter he is able to answer the questions but he has lots of pauses in what he says and it does not always sound very fluent.

Examiner comment

This student has not really thought very much about the context of this interview and how clever Capello is actually being in the interview. The student takes a purely negative view, criticising what is not being achieved, rather than looking for positives. Crucially, no actual evidence or detail from the transcript is used or referred to. This student has not yet reached grade C. It is in the D band.

C grade answer

Student B

> In this transcript Capello shows that he has learned enough English to conduct a post-match interview, which is especially hard for a manager when the team has lost. He makes it clear that he was pleased with some of the performance ('the players that played the first alf was good enough') and that he will not criticise individual players. (no no I no er I not speak about one single player).

Examiner comment

This student has a better understanding of the context of the interview and uses some examples from the data. Much of what the student says, though, describes what has been said, rather than analysing it. There is probably enough here for grade C.

When analysing transcripts like this, to get the most marks you need to go beyond describing what is happening and actually interpret and evaluate the transcript, referring to specific details. This is shown in the difference between Student A, who does not refer to a single detail from the transcript, and Student B who has referred to two specific details.

This lesson will help you to:
- explore social attitudes to language
- think about ways of collecting and sorting some data.

Social attitudes to spoken language

Social attitudes are views and opinions that are held by groups of people rather than just individuals. Although it may seem wrong to judge people by the way they speak, it does seem to happen.

Dialect and accent

The terms dialect and accent often crop up when looking at social attitudes to language. **Dialect** refers to the actual words and vocabulary that a particular group use. **Accent** refers to the way in which a particular group speaks – the particular sounds.

GradeStudio

Examiner tips

As well as dialect and accent, it is useful to know what the following terms mean:
Standard English A formal variety of spoken English which is generally taken to be free of regional characteristics in its words and grammar.
Received Pronunciation (RP) A regionally neutral accent, often associated with the educated, the upper classes and so-called important institutions such as the universities of Cambridge and Oxford.

Activity 1

Think about your own dialect and accent.

1 Write down any words you sometimes use that you would not necessarily expect to find in a school dictionary.

2 Do you pronounce any words or sounds in a particular way that is different from how others might say it?

3 What about accents and dialects other than yours? Can you think of regions that have particularly strong dialects and/or accents? Make a list. Then think what your immediate reaction is when you hear this accent or dialect.

Activity 2

Read the article opposite about how different people respond to different accents.

1 Identify the three different types of groups whose accents are mentioned here. This doesn't just mean where they are from – groups could be people of the same age or with similar backgrounds.

2 Who did the survey and why did they do it? What do we not know about the survey?

3 Think back to the work you did in Activity 1. Do you feel strongly about different accents?

The Guardian

Not all regions like to hear their own accents in ads, survey finds

Many people claim to hate the sound of their own voice, but a new government survey suggests the sensation is more unpleasant for some of us than it is for others.

The study, commissioned by the Central Office of Information (COI), reveals that, while Geordies and Mancunians enjoy listening to their own regional accents in government advertisements, Brummies and Bristolians would rather not be subjected to their own distinctive burr.

The COI found that attitudes to accents vary widely across the generations.

Older people tend to be more accepting of ad campaigns featuring received pronunciation, perhaps because they grew up listening to the "cut-glass" English accents that featured on public information films of the past.

Younger people were more engaged by local accents, it found, but sometimes a more authoritative voice is more appropriate, according to the research.

Advertisements which encourage the public to comply with deadlines, including filling in tax returns, "need to impart trust and authority" the COI said, and are more effective when a Home Counties accent is used.

Local accents proved more persuasive in campaigns which include "credible real-life experiences" to try to change people's behaviour, perhaps to prevent drink driving or encourage homeowners to fix faulty smoke alarms.

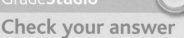

GradeStudio

Check your answer

- Did you identify the three different kinds of groups mentioned?
- Did you identify who carried out the survey and what the purpose was?
- Did you work out that the article does not tell the reader what the research methods were – who they asked, what questions and so on?

Doing a survey

One way to produce an assignment for
a survey to find out about peoples' attit
have already seen from the article on p
regional talk can bring interesting resul
ways in which different age groups spea
that you could do surveys on.

> **What annoys adults about
> teenage speakers?**

> **What annoys teenagers
> about adult criticisms of
> their speech?**

> Wh
> ha

Aquinas College Learning Centre

Customer name: Miro Kamal

Title: AQA GCSE English and English Language :
achieve a c
ID: 968758
Due: 28 October 2013

Total items: 1
07/10/2013 12:22

Thank you for using the
Library Service.

Once you have come up with a good top
method that will give you enough data to
Controlled Assessment situation.

Survey methods

When thinking about carryi
things you need to be clear

▶ **Who are you going to**
   from a particular age group, gender or social background.

▶ **What are you going to ask them? -** you need to ask
   questions which people can answer in detail. For example,
   just asking someone if they like the Geordie accent might
   not get much of a response beyond 'yes' or 'no'. Playing
   them a brief recording of Ant and Dec in the jungle, on
   the other hand, and then asking about them as presenters
   could get much more.

▶ **How will you record what they say?** - there are
   various ways to record responses, including making notes
   at the time, making sound recordings, or even asking your
   respondents to write things down for you.

GradeStudio

Examiner tip

* Be realistic about how many people
  you can ask, in what is a small study.
  Choosing three or four people could
  be enough, especially if they have
  plenty to say.

Activity 3

Take one of the examples of possible survey
topics from the speech bubbles above and
imagine you were going to carry out an actual
survey. For that topic, answer the three key
questions above – the who, what and how.

Using a questionnaire

Another way of gathering data is by doing a questionnaire. Questionnaires are similar to surveys but usually require brief answers. There can be real advantages in using them.

▶ They can be sent and returned by post, so allowing for a wider range of responses.

▶ They can lead to statistical data which can then be presented in tables and graphs.

Activity 4

Devise a questionnaire to find out what dialect words are used by your extended family.

Remember, dialect words are words used by groups of people with something in common such as:

● their region (which can also include other countries)

● their age

● their gender

● their social background.

An example would be that some Geordies use the word 'neb' for 'nose' and some people from Yorkshire say 'spice' for sweets.

To get you started, here are some common words, in their standard form, which tend to have other varieties. An example is given for each.

Standard form	Example of a dialect version
Mother	Mom
Father	Daddy
Baby	Bairn
Clever	Smarty
Superb	Mint
To tell tales	Grass
Beautiful	Lush

GradeStudio

Examiner tips

There are various ways to ask questions. In this questionnaire you could:

● give people the dialect word and ask them to say what it means

● give people the standard word and ask for a dialect version

● ask people if they actually use dialect versions as well as know them.

Writing up

Under Controlled Assessment you will need to get all your data together, ready to complete your assignment.

Let's assume you have had ten replies to your questionnaire from Activity 4. First you need to decide which bits of data you find most interesting. Then you can pull that information out and present it in an easy-to-understand format. For example, you could show the number of variations on certain words (as shown in the graph on the left), or the number of old people who use a dialect term set against young people (the graph on the right).

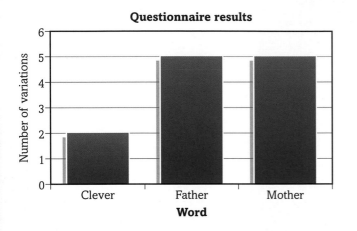

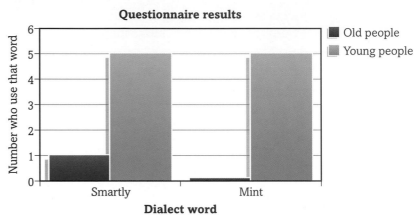

Analysing data

You will certainly gain some marks for the way you present your data, but to really impress you need to attempt to give possible analysis too. Nobody wants you to make outrageous claims from your evidence, but you do need to consider some possibilities. For example, if all old people used a dialect word, but only some younger people, why might this be so? Because the younger people have moved around the country more? Because dialects, like all language, change over time?

Activity 5

Look at the data you gathered from your questionnaire in Activity 4. Focus in on one particular part of that data and write a paragraph explaining and analysing what it shows you about language use.

Think about:

- what your data shows you
- how to interpret the data
- whether your data may possibly show something about spoken language in a wider sense.

The Grade Studio answers on page 125 will help you understand how you could structure your response.

GradeStudio

Here are two student answers to the activity on page 124. Read the answers together with the examiner comments.

Here are two student answers to the activity on page 124.

(D) grade answer

Student A

My data shows that more young people knew dialect words for 'clever' and 'mint' than old people. 5 young people used mint but no old people used or knew this word. This proves beyond doubt that old people do not use dialect words as much as young people do. This is a bit of a surprise as I thought old people would use more dialect words but my research shows the opposite is true.

Examiner comment

This student has commented on the data, but has then jumped to a whole range of conclusions when interpreting it. Phrases like 'proves beyond doubt' are very extreme when such a small sample have been questioned.

(C) grade answer

Student B

My data seems to suggest that young people are more common users of dialect words than older people are. This might be too general a statement to make though. The findings might be because, for example, the word 'mint' has a young feel to it – it would sound odd if it was used by an old person. Also, with other words there were examples where the opposite applied and old people were more common users of a certain word than young people were so really it depends on the word.

Examiner comment

This student is thoughtful, and recognises that the chosen dialect word may be to do with age rather than region – so it would be obvious that old people would not use a word that has come into use more recently.

To improve your grade when analysing data like this, you need to take account of the data's limitations as well as what it shows. The study of language does not lead to definite answers and conclusions. So, don't jump to massive conclusions based on relatively little evidence. Student A is guilty of doing this when he mistakenly writes that the data 'proves beyond doubt' his point. Instead suggest possible interpretations and even ideas for possible further data collection. This is shown in Student B's answer.

This lesson will help you to:
- think about the vast range and features of spoken genres
- consider some ways of analysing spoken genres.

Spoken genres

What is meant by 'spoken genres'?

There are many different genres of spoken language that you could write about for your assignment. In this case, 'genre' means the type of speech or text. For example, the following are all examples of spoken genres:

- school assembly
- school lesson
- public speech
- news report

- workplace meeting
- weather forecast
- interview
- TV shows where spoken language is 'represented'.

The list could go on and on, and within each genre it is possible to identify sub-genres.

GradeStudio

Examiner tips

- If you choose to do your assignment on a spoken genre, try to think of a really specific sub-genre. This will give your assignment real focus and purpose. Sub-genres can arise, for example, out of a combination of the topic (football) the circumstances (post-match), the main person involved (the manager) and the structure of the talk (interview).

GradeStudio

Check your answer

There are many possible answers here. Yours might include some of the following:
- job interview
- an interview to get into a university
- formal teacher/pupil interview
- informal teacher/pupil interview
- teacher/parent interview
- political interview on TV
- political interview on the radio
- celebrity interview on TV
- celebrity interview for a newspaper
- police interview of witness
- police interview of criminal
- voice in the street interview
- public opinion survey interview.

Activity 1

Think about the interview genre. Make a list of as many different types of interview as you can think of.

We have already seen one example with the Fabio Capello interview on page 117, so your list could begin with 'post-match interview with manager', which then might lead to 'post-match interview with player' and so on.

Features of spoken genres

If a text belongs to a particular spoken genre, this usually means it has certain rules and features. For example, in the interview genre you would always expect to see the following two features:

- one or more person(s) asking the questions (the interviewer)
- one or more person(s) replying to those questions (the interviewee).

Activity 2

1 Look at the list of spoken genres in the table below. What features would you always expect to see in each genre? Copy and complete the table. When doing this, think about:

- particular people or groups of people who must always be present in this genre
- where the spoken genre takes place
- a typical language feature that might appear in this spoken genre.

An example has been done for you.

Spoken genre	Features
Weather forecasts	a forecaster; a TV audience; a studio with weather maps; language that refers to weather, climate and predictions.
School assembly	
School lesson	
Public speech	
News report	
Workplace meetings	
Celebrity interview on TV	

Contexts

The main features of a spoken genre often remain the same. For example, an interview will always consist of someone who asks questions and someone who answers them. Where there might be variations within a spoken genre is when you start to consider the different contexts. For example, look at the different contexts for an interview below

Context	Effect
A celebrity interview on TV	Because this is a celebrity interview on TV, the main purpose for both the interviewer and interviewee is to entertain and interest the viewer. It's likely that the approach would be quite informal and the questions very friendly.
A job interview	In this context, there is a job at stake. The interviewer's main purpose is to find out information and judge personality – whether the candidate is suitable for the job. The interviewee's main purpose is to impress the interviewer. It's likely that the atmosphere will be formal and the questions quite searching.

GradeStudio

Check your answer

- For each spoken genre did you identify which people or groups of people must always be present?
- Did you identify where each spoken genre takes place?
- Did you identify typical language features of each spoken genre?

Activity 3

Take any two of the different interview sub-genres mentioned on page 126 and think about how they are different from each other. You could start with, for example, a TV interview with a politician and a police interview with a criminal. Think about how they might differ in terms of:

- their purpose
- the people involved
- the level of formality
- the potential audience for the interview.

If you choose to do your assignment on spoken genres, you could look at a transcript of something such as an interview and explore areas such as:

▶ the level of formality

▶ how questions are asked

▶ how questions are answered.

Opposite is a transcript of an interview between an adult researcher (R) and a student (S). The student attends a school in York. The researcher is making a short documentary film about some of the features of the York accent.

Read the interview, using the key to try and recreate how it might have actually sounded. Then answer the following questions.

1 Is this a formal or informal interview? How can you tell?

2 What do you notice about the questions being asked? The researcher's opening question is quite tentative. Why is this, and how does his style of questioning change as the interview goes on?

3 Interviews are often written down as records of what was said, for later reference. Write an official record of this interview. What do you notice? What kind of text does it remind you of?

Key
R = researcher
S= student
(1) = length of pause in seconds
| = when two people speak at the same time
o::: = the long vowel sound made by natives of York
? = the rising intonation that signals a question being asked

R: ccan you tell me then what some of the er distinctive features of your York accent are (1) is is it possible for you to describe them to an outsider

(2)

S: erm (1) er (1) it's it's like really strong and you can tell I'm from York and it's it's the way I say things like I'll say Yo::rk and others like I'll obviously emphasise the O in that and other people will say it differently but I can't really say that

(1)

R: so would you spot an outsider|
S: yes|

R: like me |
S: yes|

R: saying York

S: yes

R: instantly??

S: yes

R: would you?

S: yes

R: and you can tell if someone is a native of Yo::rk|
S: (laughs)|

R: is that right |
S: (laughs)|

R: by the way by the way they would say it

S: yes

Represented conversation

Another area you could explore in your assignment is scripted or 'represented' conversation. These are found in TV and radio dramas, as well as novels, short stories and other texts. It is called 'represented conversation', because it imitates the ways people speak to each other, rather than being an example of natural or real conversation.

Talk that is written to be performed is, on the page, much neater and tidier than actual talk. There are a number of reasons for this, not least the fact that scripts are written for audiences to understand.

The audience

When we watch drama, or read a novel, the conversation takes place for us – the audience – not for those who are in the drama. Sometimes the audience might know more than the characters – for example, that one character is secretly in love with another. Sometimes the audience knows less than a character – for example, a detective might typically know more than he or she let's on.

For your Controlled Assessment, you could look at an example of scripted conversation and explore some if its features. The activity below helps you get started on this area.

Activity 5

Look at this brief clip from a soap opera and answer the following questions.

1 What does the audience know that the character(s) do not?

2 How do you think pictures and actions in this script contribute to the overall drama? What effect do they have?

3 How do you react to this scene? Is it funny, sad or something else? Explain your reasons.

4 What similarities and differences does it have with real-life talk? You could compare it to the transcripts you've seen earlier in this section.

Story so far: the audience knows that Glen is keen to ask out Shelley, and that Shelley does not want to go out with him, but does not want to hurt him either.

Scene 12: Long shot of school canteen. Cut to Glen opposite Shelley at long table. Long pause with other conversation in background.

Glen: um um don't suppose you'd like to go to town Saturday (pause)
Shelley: oh oh sorry can't
Glen: Why not?
Shelley: I'm going away with my parents
Glen: Where to?
(pause – close up of Shelley thinking hard. Cut to food being eaten next to her – a pizza)
Shelley: um Italy
Glen: Italy? Just for a week-end? What are you doing there?
(through Shelley's eyes we see a female chef dolling out food)
Shelley: um my Mum's doing a cookery course for two days.
Glen: (puzzled) Ooh

GradeStudio

Check your answer

- Did you comment on what the audience knows about Glen and Shelley?
- Did you comment on how the pictures and actions heighten the drama?
- Did you explain your reaction to this scene?
- Did you compare this scripted conversation with real-life talk and notice some of the similarities ('um um') and differences (the overall flow of the conversation)?

Speeches

Another area that could provide good data to study for your assignment is the political speech. While there is no spoken interaction between people, as there is in an interview, when the speech is delivered it is important for the speaker to get some sort of response from the audience. More often than not, the main purpose of a political speech is to persuade the audience.

Activity 6

In the speech below, Prime Minister Gordon Brown talked about liberty and freedom.

1 What persuasive methods does Mr Brown use here?

2 How can you tell this is a written version of speech, rather than an actual transcript of what he said? Think of the differences between this text and the transcript on page 128.

I want to talk today about liberty – what it means for Britain, for our British identity and in particular what it means in the 21st century for the relationship between the private individual and the public realm.

I want to explore how together we can write a new chapter in our country's story of liberty - and do so in a world where, as in each generation, traditional questions about the freedoms and responsibilities of the individual re-emerge but also where new issues of terrorism and security, the internet and modern technology are opening new frontiers in both our lives and our liberties.

Addressing these issues is a challenge for all who believe in liberty, regardless of political party. Men and women are Conservative or Labour, Liberal Democrat or of some other party - or of no political allegiance. But we are first of all citizens of our country with a shared history and a common destiny.

And I believe that together we can chart a better way forward. In particular, I believe that by applying our enduring ideals to new challenges we can start immediately to make changes in our constitution and laws to safeguard and extend the liberties of our citizens:

- *respecting and extending freedom of assembly, new rights for the public expression of dissent;*

- *respecting freedom to organise and petition, new freedoms that guarantee the independence of non-governmental organisations;*

- *respecting freedoms for our press, the removal of barriers to investigative journalism;*

- *respecting the public right to know, new rights to access public information where previously it has been withheld;*

- *respecting privacy in the home, new rights against arbitrary intrusion;*

- *in a world of new technology, new rights to protect your private information;*

- *and respecting the need for freedom from arbitrary treatment, new provision for independent judicial scrutiny and open parliamentary oversight.*

Renewing for our time our commitment to freedom and contributing to a new British constitutional settlement for our generation.

GradeStudio

Check your answer

- Did you identify features of persuasive language used in the speech?
- Did you comment on how the speech lacked any of the features of actual spoken text that come across in transcripts? Or that it includes features of written language that would not appear in actual spoken language?

Here are two extracts from student answers to the activity on page 130. Read the answers together with the examiner comments.

D grade answer

Student A

> This text persuades you because it uses long words and long sentences. It says that we should all respect each other and that it doesn't matter who you vote for, we are all British together. The bullet points make a long list that make this speech easy to read.

Examiner comment

This student has not really thought very much about the fact that this is a speech, and that it is intended to be spoken aloud. The student very much responds as though this is yet another piece of work based on a written text, rather than thinking about how this could be spoken. This student has not yet reached grade C; it is heading towards a grade D.

C grade answer

Student B

> This speech uses a lot of repetition, so words like 'Britain' and 'respecting' are really important, especially if they were emphasised when they were spoken aloud. Mr Brown mentions himself a great deal and also mentions us the audience, so connecting us with what he is saying. This is therefore trying to persuade us. The long list of bullet points is a typical feature of a written text, and when spoken would not be obvious.

Examiner comment

This student has a better understanding of the fact that this is a speech, and indicates some of the key features of persuasion, such as repetition and use of pronouns. There is no real overview of what is happening here, though, so without any context the quality of the response is limited. There is probably just enough here for grade C.

When writing about formal speeches such as this one, it is best to start by providing the context of the speech, such as who is talking to whom, and why, where and when. Then it helps if you can imagine hearing the speech and consider what it would sound like. Remember too that many web sites let you hear the speech as well as read it. Student A has not thought about the speech as a spoken text – a common mistake. Student B's answer is better as she has analysed the speech as a spoken text.

This lesson will help you to:
- understand what is meant by multi-modal talk
- consider some of the ways in which people use texting to 'talk' to each other.

Multi-modal talk

What is multi-modal talk?

Traditionally language has been separated into speech and writing. New technologies mean this distinction is becoming more blurred. For example, when people 'chat' online, it could be said they are writing a form of talk. This kind of communication is an example of multi-modal talk – communication which has many of the qualities of talk, but is not actually spoken.

This section will focus on texting as a form of multi-modal talk, but there are of course many other examples that you could look at, such as instant messaging, social networking sites, emails and so on.

Activity 1

1 Make a list of all the things we do when we talk to friends and family. Think about the following when you make your list:

- The purpose of the talk – why is the conversation taking place and for what reason?
- How we sound – what we say and how we say it.
- Non-verbal communication – how do we use sounds and body language as a speaker or listener?

2 Compare your list with the one below. Are there any you missed out? Are there any you came up with not included below?

Possible purposes of talk
- to entertain – e.g. tell stories, jokes, gossip
- to make social plans
- to argue with someone
- to persuade someone

How we sound
- using informal language and slang
- at different tempos – quickly or slowly
- at different volumes – loudly or quietly
- placing emphasis on particular words

Non-verbal communication
- making expressive noises to show agreement/disagreement and other emotions
- nodding to show agreement
- smiling or laughing to show you find something funny
- using other hand and face expressions to add effect to your talk

Texting shares many of the same purposes and features of talk that you identified in Activity 1. For example, people often text to share gossip or to arrange a meet-up. Likewise, people often text using the same informal language that they would actually speak in. People also show emotion and even body language through creative use of the text system.

Activity 2

1 Below are some text messages sent by students in one class. Read the messages. For each one, see if you can say:

   a Whether it is the opening to a series of messages or a reply to a message already sent.

   b What the purpose(s) of the message is.

2 Now look at the work you did in Activity 1. Look at your own answers as well as the list provided. What do you notice about the similarities between texting and spoken language? Think about:

   - the purposes of both
   - the level of formality of both
   - what features texting uses in order to imitate some of the non-verbal features of spoken language.

Erm problies about 8 what time use going? X

U nearly ready darl? lol. x 😊

Hi hope u r ok. Hannah is off poorly. Did u sort out paying trip? See you soon, hair appt thurs 3 dec, love u, mum xxxx

Game Time! Describe me in ONE word using the third letter of YOUR name. Answer me, then forward on and see what crazy responses you get.

hey hun u'll nvr guess who I saw in twn 2day!

just wonderin if u wanted 2 come play 4 an hr. 👍

Haha consider it dun then :) awww gorge i do love you! Ur the perfect girlfriend! :) ♥ x x x x x x x x

Whos radioheads lead singer?

Just trying to sort out someone to do it for me... I wasn't told exactly if it was swine flu or not and don't want to run the risk of passing it on...!

GradeStudio

Check your answer

Look at your answer to Activity 2.

- Did you notice the shared purposes of spoken language and texting – for example, to make social plans, to request information, to gossip and so on?
- Did you notice how the language in texting is on the whole very informal – much like the language we use when we actually speak to someone?
- Did you notice how some of the text messages use emoticons and other methods to indicate non-verbal sounds and gestures?

Collecting and analysing text data

There are many ways to analyse text message data. Conveniently, all the data you might need could be on your own mobile phone – looking at a string of sent and received messages can work especially well! You could look at:

▶ texts that are similar in purpose, such as informational texts

▶ how one person uses texts – their texting 'idiolect' (the speech habits of a particular person)

▶ length of texts and whether predictive texts are longer than non-predictive

▶ methods people use to be brief when texting

▶ spelling and the use of symbolism in texts.

Activity 3

In this activity you will look at spelling and symbolism in texts. Text messaging is often criticised for its poor spelling. Another way of looking at this is to say that texters know precisely what they are doing and are in fact being creative with language – in the way poets are.

1 Look again at the text messages on page 133. Can you find any patterns to the way texters spell? Think about the following when answering this question:

● How many words are spelt correctly and how many are not?

● How are symbols used by texters to create words?

GradeStudio

Check your answer

Look at your answer to question 1.
● Did you comment on whether you thought words were spelt incorrectly on purpose?
● In doing so, did you think about the informal nature of text messaging and the need to type messages quickly?

Sounds and emotions in texting

We saw earlier that texting is a form of talk, so it needs to express sounds and emotions as well as actual words. This is all part of the multi-modal nature of text messaging.

Activity 4

Look at the four text messages below. What techniques do they use to suggest how words might be said and how the sender is feeling?

◄ Text message ►

It woz AMAZING.

◄ Text message ►

Erm I dunt know wot his problem is??? Do u?????

◄ Text message ►

That's great!!!!
C u soon

◄ Text message ►

Ha ha ha so funy its untrue

Texting controversy

Texting, and other forms of new communication, are often the subject of news stories. Many of these are negative, ranging from damage done to people's health and intelligence, to people being sacked or dumped by text. Sometimes there are good news stories involving multi-modal talk, such as miraculous surgery done by a complete novice under texted instructions from a surgeon.

GradeStudio

Check your answer

Did you comment on:
- the use of punctuation?
- the use of capitals?
- the use of 'erm' and 'ha ha'?

Activity 5

1 Search the internet for news stories involving multi-modal talk and make a collection of headlines. Make a list of advantages and disadvantages of texting mentioned in these articles.

2 Now read the 'How predictive texting takes its toll on the brain' article on page 136 and answer the following questions.

  a What statements are made about texting and its effects?

  b What evidence is used?

  c What people are named and quoted as further evidence?

  d Does the article say anything positive about texting?

  e What do you think about the claims the article makes?

You could look at the sample answers on page 137 for examples of how other students approached this question.

GradeStudio

Examiner tip

- As well as using your own data for an assignment it is also possible to look at articles such as that on page 136. If you do this, you would need to read the article closely, look carefully at its arguments and then put forward your own ideas.

Daily Mail

How predictive texting takes its toll on a child's brain

By Caroline Grant

Predictive text messaging changes the way childrens' brains work and makes them more likely to make mistakes generally, a study has found.

Scientists say the system, which involves pressing one key per letter before the phone works out what word the user wants to type, trains young people to be fast but inaccurate.

They claim this makes them prone to impulsive and thoughtless behaviour in everyday life. Modern mobile phones come with a built-in dictionary which enables them to predict what word a user wants from only a few key presses.

Each key represents three letters. It differs from an older system in which users had to hit keys several times per letter, for example pressing the 5 key three times for the letter L.

But it can lead to embarrassing miscommunications because some words use the same keys. For example, it is easy to end up asking a friend out for a quick riot (pint) or telling them about being stuck in a Steve (queue).

The study compared the mobile phone use of children aged between 11 and 14 with the results of IQ-style tests they took on computers. A quarter of the children made more than 15 calls a week and a quarter wrote more than 20 text messages a week.

Professor Michael Abramson, an epidemiologist who carried out the research, said: 'The children who used their phones a lot were faster on some of the tests but were less accurate. We suspect that using mobile phones a lot, particularly tools like predictive text, is behind this.

'Their brains are still developing so if there are effects then potentially they could impact down the line, especially given that the exposure is now almost universal. The use of mobile phones is changing the way children learn and pushing them to become more impulsive in the way they behave.' He added that the effects could have dangerous repercussions for a whole generation.

Experts concerned about the possible impact of mobile phone radiation on developing brains say that parents should be wary of allowing their children to use mobile phones too much.

But the researchers said the amount of radiation transmitted when texting is a mere 0.03 per cent of that transmitted during voice calls, suggesting radiation is not to blame for the brain effects.

Instead, Professor Abramson, from Monash University, Melbourne, believes functions such as predictive texting pose more of a risk for those whose brains are still developing.

'We don't think mobile phones are frying their brains,' he said. 'If you're used to operating in that environment and entering a couple of letters and getting the word you want, you expect everything to be like that.'

The study, which is published in the journal Bioelectromagnetics, will now be extended to look at the impact of mobile phone use on primary school children. Previous research has shown that predictive texting makes people sloppy when it comes to spelling, with many flummoxed by words such as questionnaire, accommodate and definitely.

But it is so popular that some of the mistakes that regularly crop up due to words sharing the same keys have been turned into a slang language by teenagers. They can be heard describing something as 'book' when they mean it is 'cool', for example. If a mobile phone predicts the wrong word, the user can scroll through a list of alternatives.

In 2007, a total of 57 billion text messages were sent in the UK, with 6 billion of these sent in December alone.

GradeStudio

Check your answer

- Did you list the statements about the effects of texting?
- Did you quote the evidence used in the article?
- Did you find anything positive about texting in the article?
- Did you express what you thought about the article and explain your reasons?

GradeStudio

Here are two extracts from student answers to Activity 5 on page 135. Read the answers together with the examiner comments.

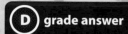

Student A

> This article says that predictive text is bad for you. 'Predictive text messaging changes the way children's brains work and makes them more likely to make mistakes generally, a study has found'. It also says that it makes children spell badly. It also says that texting makes children rush into things. I agree, as I often rush my homework.

Examiner comment

This student has not really thought very much about the way the evidence has been gathered, although they have obviously read and understood the article. The student believes all that they are told , though, and just quotes bits from the article. The personal reflection at the end does not seem very relevant. This student has not yet reached grade C. It is in the D band.

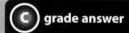

Student B

> This article makes a number of claims about predictive texting, which have been based upon an experiment with phones and IQ tests. It says that children who use predictive text a lot spell poorly, rush into things and more generally make mistakes. The findings are based on the work of an Australian professor of diseases. Personally I use predictive texting a lot myself, and it does not seem to have affected me in the way he says – but it might affect others that way.

Examiner comment

This student has a better understanding of the source of the ideas in the article although what the student says tends to describe what has been said, rather than analysing it. In the student's final sentence there is a tentative attempt to criticise some of the ideas in the article. There is probably enough here for grade C.

When criticising articles like this, to get the most marks you need to think carefully about the evidence that is put before you, and criticise it if it seems flimsy. Student A doesn't do this – he simply takes everything the article says as fact without questioning it. Student B's answer is an improvement as it begins to question the article based on the student's own experience with texting.

Exam guidance

Revision

Many students say that you can't revise for English because you don't know what the passages are that you are going to be answering on. How wrong can they be?

You need to go into the exam room with a clear sense of what you are going to have to do.

For the **Reading** section of the exam:

Make sure that you go over what features to write about if you are asked about:

▶ language

▶ presentational devices

▶ structure

▶ purpose

▶ audience.

Pick up a book, magazine or newspaper and practise looking for:

▶ the effects of language choices

▶ how the piece is structured

▶ how it is arranged on the page

▶ the effects of pictures

▶ the effects of colour

▶ the effects of other presentational devices.

Practise looking for:

▶ the main points in an argument

▶ different points the writer is making

▶ what facts there are and how the writer uses them

▶ what opinions there are and how the writer uses them

▶ any other ways that the writer supports the points being made.

GradeStudio

Examiner tip

- There are 120 minutes for the exam and 80 marks, so that works out at one and a half minutes per mark. It's easy then to work out how many minutes you should spend on each question. For example:
  4 marks = 6 minutes
  6 marks = 9 minutes
  8 marks = 12 minutes
  16 marks = 24 minutes
  24 marks = 36 minutes.
  If you do this, then you will give yourself the best chance.
  Do well!

For the **Writing** section of the exam:

Keep saying to yourself over and over again:

▶ plan

▶ write

▶ check.

Make sure that you do all three in the exam room.

Go over common mistakes that you make:

▶ in spelling

▶ in grammar

▶ in punctuation

▶ in sentence structure.

When you get into the exam room:

▶ don't be in too much of a hurry

▶ read the question several times

▶ underline the key words of the task

▶ do exactly what you are asked to do

▶ spend your time wisely and stick to your time allocations.

Sample Foundation tier exam paper

English/English Language

(Specification A)
FOUNDATION

Unit 1 Understanding and producing non-fiction textss

Time allowed
- 2 hours

Answer **all** questions

Section A: Reading

Answer **all** questions

You are advised to spend about one hour on this section.

Read Item 1, *Daily Star Says...* and answer the question below.

1 Give four reasons why, according to the *Daily Star,* Britain should host the World Cup.　　*(4 marks)*

Now read Item 2, *After 400 years, stepladders are banned from Oxford's library* and answer the question below.

2 How do the views of the Health and Safety Officer differ from those of some of the library's users?　　*(4 marks)*

Now read Item 3, *2012: The Slummer Olympics*, and answer the questions below.

3 Which facilities did the investigators find to be sub-standard and what was wrong with each of those facilities?　　*(8 marks)*

4　Find and write down four examples of interesting uses of language in Item 3 and explain what the effect of each of them is.　　*(12 marks)*

Now look at **all three** items.

5 Choose **two** of the items.

　　Compare the effect on the reader of some of the presentational devices used.　　*(12 marks)*

Section B: Writing

Answer **both** questions in this section.

You are advised to spend about one hour on this section.

You have received the following email from Mrs Mary Samuelson, the Deputy Head.

From: msamuelson@hotmail.com

cc. Year 11 students

Re: Information Sheet

Dear Student,

I am writing to ask you to create an Information
Sheet to be given to new Year 7 pupils,
informing them about health and safety issues
in the school and advising them of the best ways
of staying healthy and safe while at school.

Yours sincerely,

Mary Samuelson

7 Reply in a formal email, letting her know when you can produce the
   Information Sheet by and outlining what you are going to include in it.   (*16 marks*)

8 Write the Information Sheet.   (*24 marks*)

Item 1

DAILY STAR Says...

We are up for the cup

Britain must host the World Cup again.

It's been far too long since the ultimate football tournament was played here.

We are the most passionate soccer-loving nation on the planet.

And with international superstars like David Beckham and Wayne Rooney championing our cause, there's only one place the 2018 World Cup should be held.

The England idols headed a star-studded ceremony yesterday, helping to kick-start our bid to host the event in nine years' time.

They were backed by big hitters Prince William and Gordon Brown.

Let's hope this slick presentation will be followed up by a real push to secure the tournament.

We are the perfect country to run for this cup. We have state-of-the-art stadia, the world's best players and a history rich in footballing tradition.

As Wills said, football is in our blood.

We're well overdue the chance to show that to the world.

Item 2

After 400 years, stepladders are banned from Oxford's library

STEPLADDERS have been banned from part of Oxford University's historic Bodleian library – because of health and safety fears.

The ruling by officials means that students cannot use items on the higher shelves of the Duke Humfrey reading room.

However, the university is standing its ground and refusing to move the books from their 'original historic location' on the room's balcony.

As a result of the stalemate, students have to travel to libraries as far away as London to view other copies.

Art History student Kelsey Williams, 21, had to travel 80 miles to London to view a copy of Arthur Johnston's 1637 work Delitiae Poetarum Scotorum after librarians

Treacherous: The gallery of Duke Humfrey's reading room

refused to get it down for her. She said: 'Access to these books is necessary for my research and I wasted a day travelling to London and looking at the one in the British Library.

'It's madness because I can practically see the Bodleian's copy every time I walk into Duke Humfrey's.'

Stepladders have been used by scholars to reach books since the library was built more than 400 years ago.

But the University's Health and Safety officer put his foot down last year and they were removed two weeks ago.

A notice given to students requesting the books reads: 'Unable to fetch, book kept on top shelf in gallery. Due to new health and safety measures, stepladders can no longer be used.'

Laurence Benson, the library's director of administration and finance, said: 'The balcony has a low rail and we have been instructed by the health and safety office that this increases the risk.

'As part of the process the restriction on the use of ladders on the balcony have been introduced.

'The library would prefer to keep the books in their original historic location – where they have been safely consulted for 400 years prior to the instructions from the Health and Safety office.'

Daily Mail

Four months after all this...

...our hopes for glory in 4yrs on home soil look like THIS

CRACKED: Tooting track

PEOPLE INVESTIGATION

BRITAIN was last night shamed by the ghetto-style sports sites set to host the world's best athletes at the 2012 Olympics.

■ **By DANIEL JONES**

Games chiefs proudly unveiled in May the 96 venues picked to be used as training camps by legends including cyclist Chris Hoy and Jamaican sprinter Usain Bolt.

But months after stars like swimmer Rebecca Adlington took Team GB's medal tally to 47 in Beijing, the next generation of heroes face facilities like slums.

Among the horrors were a dangerously sub-standard running track, mouldy showers and excrement-splattered toilets.

Olympics minister Tessa Jowell and games chief Lord Sebastian Coe trumpeted the sports centres chosen across the capital as 'high quality facilities' which met tough criteria.

They will be used by the international elite in the run-up to their events at the summer Olympics

when the world's eyes are on Stratford, East London, and its outposts. But a spot-check of the Linford Christie Outdoor Sports Centre, Wormwood Scrubs, West London, found a rubble-strewn site with rusting, stomach-churning changing rooms. And the training facilities were submerged in water, overgrown and forgotten.

Meanwhile, the surface at Tooting Bec Athletics Track nearby was cracked and lifting. White Hart Lane Community Centre in North London was shabby and neglected, as was Barn Elms Sports Centre, South West London.

A spokesman for the London 2012 Organising Committee said: 'Many of these facilities have funding in place and, as most teams will not come to train until 2011, there is time for work to take place.'

2012: THE SLUMMER OLYMPICS

Shock pictures show state of facilities for next generation

HOLEY INADEQUATE: White Hart nets

TAPPED: Tottenham showers fit criteria

BRICKBATS: Rubble at 'quality' venue

PREMIER DIVISION: Rusty roller and boarding by broken bleachers at White Hart Lane

NO LOVE LOST: Neglected tennis courts in South West London

Sample Higher tier exam paper

English/English Language

(Specification A)
HIGHER

Unit 1 Understanding and producing non-fiction texts

Time allowed
• 2 hours

Answer **all** questions

Section A: Reading

Answer **all** questions

You are advised to spend about one hour on this section.

Read Item 1, *Bring back the beaver – he will save money and clean our rivers'*, and answer the question below.

1 What, according to the article, are the advantages and disadvantages of beavers?   (*8 marks*)

Now read Item 2, *Seasonal stray-dog crisis*, and answer the question below.

2 How do the picture, the headline and other presentational devices contribute to the effectiveness of this text?   (*8 marks*)

Now read Item 3, an extract from a prose work by the poet Gillian Clarke, and answer the question below.

3 How does Gillian Clarke reveal her attitudes and feelings in this passage?   (*8 marks*)

Now look at **all three** items.

4 Look at Item 3 and **either** of the other items.

Compare the ways language is used for effect in the two texts.   (*16 marks*)

Section B: Writing

Answer **both** questions in this section.

You are advised to spend about one hour on this section.

5 You have been asked to contribute to a collection of pieces of writing where the writers choose a moment from their past which was really important to them.

Write about such a moment and explain its importance to you. (*16 marks*)

6 Your local newspaper has been running a campaign recently about your local council wasting public money on causes that some people think are trivial.

Choose a cause which you care about and write an article justifying spending public money on it. (*24 marks*)

THE TIMES

Bring back the beaver – he will save money and clean our rivers

Valerie Elliott Countryside Editor

The return of beavers to England after being hunted to near-extinction in the country 400 years ago could help hard-pressed households by bringing down water bills.

According to an independent scientific study, beavers are natural engineers and help to clean rivers and prevent flooding. Their presence would save spending on expensive treatment works and other flood defences as well as the benefit of lower charges, researchers say.

The study for Natural England, the Government's wildlife advisers, and the People's Trust for Endangered Species, raises the prospect of an eventual return of this shy, nocturnal creature to almost any English river, even the western reaches of the Thames in London.

Resistance comes from landowners and farmers concerned about damage to trees and culverts, the spread of disease, a rise in sightseers traipsing

Online

Read our dedicated environment blog

timesonline.co.uk/greencentral

Beavers: 'No threat to human health'

over private land and hefty costs for fencing.

But despite the opposition, South West Water is keen to use beavers to help to purify drinking water. Researchers point to their role in creating upstream ponds that capture sediment and other organic matter. Other benefits are identified in terms of biodiversity, with cleaner waters providing improved conditions for fish spawning.

John Gurnell, a wildlife biologist at Queen Mary, University of London, who led the research, described beavers as 'ecosystem engineers'. He said: 'The potential for them to give benefits to the country at large is quite enormous.' Water quality, the effects of flooding and river levels during drought would all be helped, with the added hope of lower bills, he added.

He wanted the study to demolish the myth about beavers. 'Most negative effects are probably more minor than major,' he said. He denied that beavers were a threat to human health.

'We don't recommend hugging beavers even though they are mild-mannered, gentle and docile, but they have teeth,' he said.

Even though beavers largely died out in England in the 16th century, a few natives survived until the 1900s and about 40 are in captivity at five locations. They live in the wild in most of Europe, however, and in Vienna they live on river banks near the city.

The most likely scenario for a comeback in England is to introduce three of four families – about twenty beavers – on a single site. Costs could top £1 million. Best-suited areas for a colony are along river banks in the Weald of Kent, the New Forest, Bodmin Moor, the Peak District and Forest of Bowland.

● Freedom may be short-lived for a beaver that escaped from a farm in Devon in October and set up home on the banks of the River Tamar. Derek Gow, a conservationist, says he plans to lure the beaver into a trap with scent from an imported female and return him to his enclosure.

Item 2

THE TIMES

The Dogs Trust has offered advice to pet owners: feed dry food instead of tinned, insure your pet – and avoid costly accessories such as sparkly collars

Seasonal stray-dog crisis comes early as families abandon pets to save cash

Fiona Hamilton
London Correspondent

Luxuries were the first things to go: foreign holidays, expensive Christmas presents, office parties. Now Rufus, Spot and Max, along with many of their furry brethren, are the latest victims of the financial crisis.

Dog charities have reported an unprecedented number of stray animals after the credit crunch, with families forsaking their pets to save money.

Battersea Dogs & Cats Home announced yesterday that it had almost reached capacity – for the first time – because of the high number of strays and lost animals being brought in. The Dogs Trust, the country's largest dog welfare charity, told *The Times* that it was experiencing a similar trend.

Animal charities are used to coping with spikes in demand after Christmas, when new pets turn from a novelty into an unwanted gift, but the deluge this year has come a month early.

The Battersea home, in southwest London, has taken 6,430 stray dogs this year, compared with 5,335 by the same time in 2007. Strays account for more than 80 per cent of its dogs.

The charity attributed the high number of strays to the credit crunch, as well as the impact of new legislation that has led to fewer owners being reunited with their

Hounded by costs

- £13,000 – the average cost of keeping a dog over its lifetime; 24 per cent higher than in 2000
- The annual cost of between £710 and £810 includes:
- £150 on dog food
- £100 on grooming
- £120 on insurance
- £30 for deworming
- £20 for defleaing
- £140 for two weeks at a kennel
- The one-off cost of neutering is between £150 and £250

Source: Intune pet insurance provider

lost dogs.

Jan Barlow, chief executive of the home, said it appeared that many owners whose animals had strayed were not actively looking for them, because of financial pressures.

She added: '[The increase] could be because people can't afford to keep their dogs any more, so are dumping them on the streets.

'For those who cannot look after their dog or cat because they cannot afford to keep them, we urge them to contact Battersea, or their local rescue centre, rather than dumping them or allowing them to stray.'

People are also more reluctant to take on the cost of adopting a pet, with the Dogs Trust experiencing greater difficulties than usual in rehoming strays. At the charity's centre in West London, it is taking as long as six months to rehome dogs, whereas under usual circumstances they would be found homes within three months.

The trust offered advice to dog owners wishing to cut costs, suggesting that they feed their pets dry food instead of tinned, and buy dog food in bulk rather than as part of the weekly shop. It also suggests taking out pet insurance so that vet bills are not overwhelming, and avoiding over-the-top pet accessories such as sparkly collars.

Ms Barlow expressed concern that, after the implementation of legislation in April, many owners did not know where to find their lost dogs.

Under the Clean Neighbourhoods and Environment Act, stray dogs were made the responsibility of local authorities, whereas previously they were taken to the police.

Ms Barlow said: 'If you've lost your dog, you could be reunited with it in time for Christmas by contacting your local authority.'

I try to ignore Christmas. It all starts too soon. I hate the bling, the cheap glitter, the unremitting materialism, the waste, the flashing lights, the destruction of rural darkness by the spreading disease of giant illuminated nodding Santas and snowmen and, God help us, flashing inflatable cribs. I want an airgun for Christmas so that I can shoot Santa Claus and watch him deflate with a hiss. Lights fidget on houses all the way from Ceredigion to Cardiff, eating the ozone layer and melting the Greenland glaciers. Where is the romance of the one lit tree in the window we used to count on winter walks with the kids? Bah! Humbug!

I have a theme for the Cardiff poem, but they won't like it. The winter solstice. The darkest night. The year's midnight. We brazen out the narrowing days with light. Out there in the temperate city an ice rink glitters on a civic lawn as if we dreamed Victorian glitter when lakes were dancing floors, the rivers froze for goose fairs and all was marble winter. For now, the city puts on party clothes. We say, dress every tree with electricity. Switch on the lights. Let streets and houses glow. When the party's over, and we step into the night and feel the Ice Queen's wand of cold, an imagined hush of snow will touch the heart, and we'll know that for the pleasures of here and now we are borrowing bling from the glacier, slipping Greenland's shoulder from its wrap of snow.

> Oh, ice-makers, who can make a frozen floor
> in the maritime air of our mild city,
> bring your alchemy to the melting permafrost.
>
> Chain the glacier. Put the wilderness under locks.
> Rebuild the gates of ice. Hold back the melt-water
> for footfall of polar bear and Arctic fox.[1]

Fast forward again to the now of a cold, dry December. Frost glitters on the sandstone terrace, and on the hedge banks frost stays white all day. The slate table is laid with glitter. I put a red enamel plate of crumbs on its cloth-of-silver for the robins, who do not like the bird feeder. The birds are getting through all the seed, nuts, crumbs, bacon fat, cheese rind I can give them – sacks of it. There are treecreepers in the plum trees, a greater spotted woodpecker on the nut holder. The white-collared female blackbird sees off two male competitors for food – or is she displaying her spirit and resourcefulness, ready for spring mating?

We walk hard-frozen ground to check and count the sheep. One year, before Christmas we lost a yearling ram. Accurately counting sheep can be difficult. The little ram may have got under a gate. By the time we found him he had been alone for weeks. He was thin and weak, found wandering at the far end of the wood where no sheep ought to have been. We brought him home, fed him, gave him shelter for a few days, and he improved. We kept him in the field closest to the house, and watched him grazing there, thinking he'd make it. But sheep are strange animals. They don't thrive on their own. They are flock creatures and seem to lose the will to live when away from their kind. One day we could not see him grazing in the field. He had found a corner to die in. The wool torn from his fleece by the crows lay scattered on the grass for months. It was later taken by nesting birds. Nothing goes to waste in nature. That winter our Christmas cards used his story, and a photograph of our midsummer hayfield. The poem expected him to live. The words celebrate his response to us, the slow improvement in his strength, and the good sight of him pulling clean hay from the manger. By Christmas he had changed his mind and lost heart, and one night he lay down in the field to die. Such failures always hurt. As children we learn the pain of the loss of animals: guinea pigs, hamsters, birds saved from the jaws of a cat. But it still hurts.

---

[1] 'Solstice' (unpublished).